THE HEART OF A HEALTHY BODY

Herbert Beuoy

Helping People Find
Healing and Wholeness
through the Body of Christ

Healing Ministry within the Local Church

UPPER
ROOM BOOKS

NASHVILLE

The Heart of a Healthy Body

All the stories in this book are true. Some of the names and details have been changed to avoid embarrassment or discomfort for the persons described.

Scripture quotations not otherwise identified are from the *Holy Bible: New International Version*. Copyright © 1973, 1978, 1984 International Bible Society. Used by permission of Zondervan Bible Publishers.

Scripture quotations designated RSV are from the Revised Standard Version of the Bible, copyrighted 1946, 1952, and © 1971 by the Division of Christian Education, National Council of Churches of Christ in the United States of America, and are used by permission.

Scripture quotations from *The New Testament in Modern English*, by J. B. Phillips, are reprinted by permission of the Macmillan Company. Copyright © 1958 by J. B. Phillips.

Scripture quotations designated KJV are from the King James Version of the Bible.

Cover Design: Steve Laughbaum
First Printing: November 1988 (5)
Library of Congress Catalog Card Number: 88-050243
ISBN: 0-8358-0587-5

Printed in the United States of America

This book is dedicated—with heartfelt praise and gratitude to the God of all healing—to the Wednesday evening healing team at Central United Methodist Church, Decatur, Illinois.

Contents

Introduction

Salvation, Healing, and Wholeness

I saw a bumper sticker announcing one of Kathryn Kuhlman's favorite statements, "I believe in miracles." *Good for you,* I thought sarcastically. *I believe in God.*

Miracle is a turn-off word for millions of responsible Christians. When we think of healing, we think of miracles; and that triggers latent resistance to the popular concept of healing as miracle.

I believe in God, but I'm no longer uncomfortable with the term *miracle*. There are other words, however, that may carry more freight and arouse less antipathy. We'll come to them shortly.

I can't tell you how to produce a miracle. I'm hard pressed even to define one. The God in whom I believe relates to us children regularly in terms of loving, nurturing intervention. To us is given the privilege, challenge, and risk of venturing in faith to discover how to cooperate with God in receiving and recognizing divine action in our lives.

Some people think of miracles as occurrences that function by as-yet-undiscovered natural law. Bring a seventeenth-century scientist into a twentieth-century home, press a button on a wall, and see light radiate from a fixture in the ceiling. That scientist thinks it's a miracle! But the seventeenth century had never heard of electricity.

Other people see miracles as events from a children's storybook in which the fairy godmother touches a physical object with a star-tipped wand. In a starburst of glory the frog is changed into a prince or an acorn is changed into a diamond.

There is a major biblical theme that includes, but far transcends, the concept of miracle. Salvation. Salvation is not complete in any of us until we reach the wholeness God intends for all people.

Unbelief and Unreality

In western culture most of us are programmed by excellent educational procedure to think in terms of observable cause and effect. Whatever is outside the space-time continuum is disregarded because it is not subject to scientific scrutiny. Some people go so far as to say that whatever is outside the space-time continuum is nonexistent. That in itself is an affirmation of faith.

Faith is also the basis for believing that the Lord of creation has reserved the privilege of entering into natural process to make changes. Changes that defy normal cause-and-effect explanations are not necessarily miracles. They may be only manifestations of natural law not yet discovered by humankind.

On the other hand, it would be presumptuous to explain away every purported instance of divine intervention by saying it was simply natural process of a law not yet discovered or of a higher order. I prefer to reserve *miracle* to refer to the direct intervention of God's power to accomplish something which, without that intervention, would not occur.

There are two primary ways in which this benign intrusion of the God of love is thwarted. One is to disallow theologically that God acts in such ways in our era. This is inadequate faith, maybe even unbelief. The other is to be indiscriminate in ballyhooing every emotionally induced change as a miracle. This is unrealistic faith. Perhaps it could be called distorted belief. We'll address these issues more thoroughly later.

The God of creation and redemption is steadfast, dependable, unchanging. God is also the One who has entered history in a decisive, "miraculous" way through birth by a human mother. God is the One who was crucified, dead, buried, and rose again on the third day. God can enter history—even our history—with or without our permission. (The intentional ministry of healing, incidentally, is nothing more than a conscious effort to allow God freedom for that entry.) When God does so, it might be called a miracle. God's doing, not ours.

An Intentional Ministry of Healing

The intentional ministry of healing in a local church is the "heart" of a healthy body. This is true because the purpose of the church is to re-present

Jesus Christ in this age. The continuous work of Jesus Christ is to bring salvation, healing, and wholeness to a dying world. That's the very heart of our task.

There is another sense in which the healing ministry is the heart of the local church. It is an interior ministry. It is not the tail that wags the dog. It is one ministry among many in the Lord's work. But, like my heart and yours, it simply beats behind the scenes of its own accord. You don't have to kick it to keep it going. It keeps right on beating whether it gets "strokes" of encouragement or not.

Furthermore, it is not in itself the saving power. As the heart pumps life-carrying blood to all the extremities of the body, so the faith-expressing ministry of healing "pumps" the saving reality of God's healing love into the Body of Christ. The intentional ministry of healing is the heart of a healthy body.

In every local church where the life and love of Jesus are being experienced, people are growing in salvation, healing, and wholeness. They may not use those terms to describe it, but that's not important. A rose by any other name smells as sweet.

There are three reasons for entering into an intentional ministry of healing in addition to the spontaneous growth toward wholeness that a live Body of Christ generates by its very existence. In addition to exploring these reasons, this book will consider some of the objections to the ministry of healing. Many Christians who believe that there are excellent biblical and experiential grounds for healing are convinced that it would be counterproductive to officially designate such a ministry in the local church.

Objections to the Ministry of Healing

One of the main objections to a healing ministry is the possibility of promising that which can't be delivered. What happens to the faith of persons who come expectantly for healing and find no relief for their symptoms? More damage may be done among those who are disappointed than benefits accrue to those who are healed.

I know a teenage boy who threw his glasses away to demonstrate faith that his eyes had been healed. This bold action was taken at the instruction of the "healer," who told him to prove his faith by going without glasses. Positive faith declarations and "demonstrations" of confidence in healing have often exacerbated rather than alleviated ill health.

Some proponents of healing insist that all illness is the result of personal sin. Think of the negative impact on people who are given to unresolved guilt—in addition to the physical suffering they might be experiencing—by a vain search for that particular sin for which God is punishing them.

In some popularized expressions of the ministry of healing there is a disturbing commercialism, reminiscent of Madison Avenue hype, that tends to diminish the sense of awe and majesty that we wish reserved for the sovereign God of the universe. Other systems of healing are couched in faddish clichés. Many of them appear to be based on a placebo effect. It sometimes seems that the faithful are more urged to psych themselves up than to trust the Lord Jesus.

The ministry of healing, whatever its level of integrity, is vividly presented to the public through

TV, radio, and print. Much of what the average Christian perceives, presented without adequate theological basis, raises suspicion and distrust in the minds of people. A careful re-education of members will help avoid misunderstanding in any congregation that decides to implement an intentional ministry of healing.

Reasons for Considering an Intentional Ministry of Healing

The reasons for considering an intentional ministry of healing in the local church begin with a biblical understanding of the nature of the church as the Body of Christ. As the Body of Christ we take our model of activity from what he did and what he told his followers to do.

"Jesus went through all the towns and villages, teaching in their synagogues, preaching the good news of the kingdom and healing every disease and sickness" (Matt. 9:35). This is a comprehensive statement that is repeated several times in the Gospels. More compelling, however, is the fact that a large number of the incidents recorded by the Gospel writers are stories about the compassion of Jesus manifested through the healing of persons. Many of our churches follow Jesus' example in teaching and preaching but fail to explore the third major facet of his ministry, that of healing.

Not only did Jesus model the ministry of healing for his disciples but he also instructed them to do so. "When Jesus had called the Twelve together, he gave them power and authority to drive out all demons and to cure diseases, and he sent them out to preach the kingdom of God and to heal the sick" (Luke 9:1-2). Jesus practiced the ministry of healing and instructed his disciples to "heal the sick."

In later chapters we will examine the way in which the early church, after its infusion of power from the Pentecost experience—which is in full force today— also practiced the ministry of healing in obedience to Christ. The first reason for establishing a ministry of healing in our churches is out of simple obedience to the Lord of the church, the head of the Body of Christ.

From another perspective there is an even more compelling reason for offering the ministry of healing. We have multitudes of people with illnesses in our society. Most of them could be helped perceptibly by an influx of the life and love of Jesus. It's true that those outside the church are unlikely to look to us for help. That's because they are unaware the church offers a ministry of healing.

However, we don't have to look outside our congregations for people to heal. Once our ministry of healing begins in our own ranks, the word will spread to those on the outside that the healing love of God is available among us. The second major reason for considering an intentional ministry of healing in the local church is that we can provide salvation, healing, and wholeness for hurting people through such a program.

One of the major goals of this book is to encourage the current healthy trend in many of our churches: the increase of the ministry of the laity and the priesthood of all believers. An important lesson to come out of the charismatic renewal is that the laity are no longer satisfied to sit back and let the professionals do all the ministry. They want a piece of the action. This is the third major reason for considering a ministry of healing.

The title phrase "a healthy body" will be emphasized, described, and encouraged in this book. It is assumed that churches of vital, exuberant health are equipping the laity to carry out ministries of many kinds. No ministry is more suited to use the gifts, compassion, and faith of the laity than that of healing.

Most laypersons are sensitive to the pervasive need for the ministry of healing. Some of them are gifted by God for this ministry. When they are given the opportunity to receive thorough training and oversight as part of a healing team, they will respond with eagerness.

At the same time, this will broaden the deeper understanding of salvation, healing, and wholeness among members of the congregation. Many laypersons who become part of the ministry will be ardent and careful exponents of legitimate faith principles for the healing ministry.

Would your church benefit from inaugurating an intentional ministry of healing? The Lord of the church requires it. The hurting people of the world need it. Many Christian laypersons are gifted and called to that ministry. Now may be the time to consider a ministry which is the heart of a healthy body.

CHAPTER 1

Skepticism

"That's him," Jack said. "The one in the vest."
Three men had just entered the lounge area. The
one in the vest, according to Jack's story, had been
"miraculously healed" of multiple sclerosis. Now he
was one of the leaders for this weekend spiritual
retreat. How did I get talked into this unwelcome
weekend experience? It was not even a comfortable
getaway. The place was depressing. A former con-
vent in a semi-commercial area of the city, it was
dirty red brick outside, on the inside warped,
creaky wood flooring and drab, cream-colored walls
that had been neither washed nor painted for de-
cades. The sleeping rooms were box-sized. I was
squeezed into one of these two-cot boxes with Jack
by random assignment.

Jack, it turns out, was a talker, a nonstop support-
er of these retreat weekends. Gene Harbison—he of
the multiple sclerosis miracle—had been verbal ex-

hibit A. There he stood, not thirty feet from me.
Gene Harbison—live!

He didn't look like a miracle to me. Trim and a
little above average height, he stood casually and
slightly stooped. He wore a bright red vest, which
was apparently some sign of leadership status.
Otherwise undistinguished, he stood listening
quietly to the conversation of his friends.

On the other hand, I didn't know what a miracle
was *supposed* to look like. As far as I knew at the time,
I'd never seen one. An irreverent thought from a
childhood poem popped into my mind. "I can tell
you anyhow, I'd rather see than be one."

These derogatory feelings about healing miracles
surprised me. I had considered myself open-minded
on the subject of healing. Intrigue or curiosity
would have been more in order.

Men were still arriving, many sharing jovial, hug-
ging reunions with one another while room assign-
ments were being made. I decided to take a walk.

Healing: (semi)Pro and Con(job)?

A few weeks earlier I had sat in a little cafe booth
with two other pastors joined in heated debate over
the ministry of healing. For one, it was a question of
integrity. For the other, a matter of uncertain faith. I
was the one in the group leaning toward beginning
such a ministry.

Jesus had clearly sent out his disciples to teach,
preach, *and* heal. His own ministry, which we
sought to emulate, as well as these instructions to
his immediate followers, not only provided us with
a model but also commanded us by extension to be

about the ministry of healing. Our denomination had been big on teaching and preaching. For the most part, however, we had thought and acted as if there were no such gospel mandate as healing. I said simple obedience required us to explore healing as a normative part of the pastoral ministry.

Now I found myself in a perplexing midair swoosh on the reverse pendulum swing. I was big on doctrine. Face to face with the claim of a miracle, I was anything but secure. Some faith in healing!

Sedgewick, the younger of the two pastors with me, argued for integrity and valid theology. This discussion on healing seemed to have tapped a sour vein of bitterness in him. At one point his face got red; his eyes glistened. Even now I remembered his clipped words with a slight chill. "People who run healing shows do it for one reason and one reason only. They're after the bucks." I doubted there was anything consciously fraudulent about Jack or Gene Harbison. I wondered if this weekend would provide me the opportunity for discovering whether or not this "healing" was valid.

The other man in the booth that day was wistful. Only a few years from retirement, he wondered if his generation of pastors had missed offering their people something profound from the very core of the gospel message. As with me, however, it was primarily theoretical. He had never really seen a miracle. What happens to people, he mused, when you convince them to exercise faith for healing? You go through all the right biblical procedures. You pronounce appropriate incantations. You believe. And nothing appears to change. What happens to your credibility in their eyes? What happens to their faith in a loving God? Perhaps worse, what happens to their sense of personal self-worth, no doubt already diminished by the illness or injury that evinced the need for healing?

Some ministers of healing seemed able to leap that problem with facile grace. Dr. Lawrence Lacour told me of the dialogue he had with Oral Roberts. Lacour, who had an impressive reputation as a preacher and teacher of preaching in the United Methodist church, was entering retirement after a long pastorate at the prestigious First United Methodist Church in Colorado Springs. Oral Roberts University wanted him to teach young preachers in its school of theology.

At one point in the interview with President Roberts, Lacour mentioned what he thought was a telling flaw in his suitability for the job. "Oral, I've never prayed for anybody's healing in my whole life."

"Why not?"

"I'm concerned about what would happen to them if they weren't healed."

"Oh, I've prayed for more people than anyone else in the world who haven't been healed!"

"Then why do you do it?"

"Because some are healed. Some are!"

A Context for Manipulation?

It was easy for me to empathize with Sedgewick. Earlier that year I had suffered through a miserable evening of manipulation at the hands of a pair of nationally publicized charismatic evangelists. They were flamboyant on TV and color photographed in full-page magazine ads; popular books flowed from their pens; and they were coming to a city near the town in which I pastored!

Leaders of the local chapter of Aglow (for which I was one of the advisory pastors) and members of the Full Gospel Business Men's Association were ecstatic. They planned for weeks to arrange for several carloads of excited followers to make the drive to the huge auditorium for this great rally. Understandably, those from the church I served were eager that their pastor should benefit from this rare opportunity to experience the power of God. I climbed into a large luxury car for the trip, an honored, but anxious, guest passenger.

We arrived an hour early, the better to get choice seats. There we sat, rows 14 and 15 from the platform, comprising a neat little representative block from our hometown. We waited with patient enthusiasm, sharing charismatic clichés in that jovial fashion suited to encourage others and, perhaps, convince ourselves that we were properly "in the Spirit," ready to praise the Lord.

At last the service began. We sang exuberant praise songs. We clapped our hands and stomped our feet. We raised our hands to the Lord and really got with it. A little of this style of worship goes a long way with me, but the active involvement greatly reduced my level of tension.

Our esteemed leaders were definitely show-business types. They were relaxed and used a lot of humor to warm us up. There was more than exuberance here. Godliness was shining through. I was beginning to enjoy the evening.

Gradually they led us into a holier and more

serious mood. They were preparing us for the awesome ministry of a powerful God. I perceived clear
evidence of sincerity as they witnessed to times
when they had failed God by counting too much on
themselves rather than trusting God. Tonight they
wanted to be totally dependent on God's power, not
their own. My irreverent mind flashed a ludicrous
memory verse called Glyme's Formula for Success
into consciousness. "The secret of success is
sincerity. Once you can fake that, you've got it
made." My ambivalence was showing.

At this juncture one of the leaders began to tell us
how wonderful pastors are. "We just *love* our pastors," she said, her arms stretched out to indicate a
loving embrace for all these amazing people. "How
we thank God for these wonderful men." A win-
some smile. "How many pastors do we have here
tonight? Won't you please stand so we can see who
these wonderful men are?" She began to applaud
and nod her head in encouragement for the crowd
to join in honoring their wonderful pastors.

This is a setup for something, I thought. But what
could I do? All around me were parishioners who
loved me and wanted the best for me. They wanted
me to stand and be recognized for the important
task to which the Lord had called me.

I wanted to slump further into the upholstered
theater seat. I thought I was being flattered and
pandered to in an obviously manipulating ploy, and
I doubted if more than one or two of the people from
our town realized that. I began to feel angry. I stood.
I halfway smiled to mas the expression of anger. I
sat down again, wondering what the next step
would be.

This moment of honor occurred about half an hour into the meeting. I was to wait another hour before the payoff came. In the meantime we were treated to a steady stream of "miracles."

The Miracles Begin

A long line of sufferers who desired prayer waited for their moment of ministry. It appeared that when they reached the healers at center stage they were asked the nature of the problem. From our place in the audience we could not hear the conversation, though sometimes the leaders would lean over to the standing mike and report it to all of us. Depending on the answer, the leaders put their hands on the afflicted portion of the body or on the forehead and prayed. Many of those who were prayed for slumped backward in a dead faint, a phenomenon about which my college and seminary training had left me uninformed. I had since learned, however, to recognize this as being "slain in the Spirit" or "falling under the power."

Another amazing demonstration of God's mysterious work was the "word of knowledge." Every few minutes one of the leaders went to the microphone to announce a work of God being accomplished in that very moment for whomever had faith to claim the word for his or her condition. "There is a problem with a knee," he announced casually, almost offhandedly. "Someone here has a knee that's been bothering them." He paused, then continued a little haltingly. "I seem to see it was injured in a fall." (*Someone? There must be thirty bad knees in this crowd,* I thought.)

The person in question, it turned out, was very near me, two rows closer to the platform, in the end seat. He stood in the aisle, gingerly bending the knee. Then he began pulling it to a more acute angle. He swung it back and forth, faster and faster. Then he bounced away on a brisk walk up and down the aisle. Healed by the power of God. The audience cheered and applauded, praising God.

Yet another kind of miracle was much in evidence. Many of those who told their needs to the leaders were asked to stretch out their arms perpendicular to their body directly in front of themselves and bring the palms of the hands lightly together. If the fingertips of one hand extended beyond the other, it was necessary to "command" the shorter arm to grow out. In variant situations this same remedy might also be applied to the lower extremities. The sufferer would sit on a chair or on the floor. The relative length of the legs would be determined. One of the evangelists would issue the command, and the shorter leg lengthened. The miracle healing was accomplished and announced. Everyone praised God with cheers and applause.

In these circles, "falling under the power" was seen as an awesome manifestation of God's power, a sure way to know that *God*, not mere humanity, was in control. Manifest physical changes such as perceptible lengthening of arms or legs were purported to be external evidence that inner changes, perhaps not immediately discernible, were also occurring, to the glory of God ("Give the Lord a great big hand"; enthusiastic applause) and the professed well-being of the sick or injured person.

Pastors Put on the Spot

Person after person had fallen "under the power."
Our reknowned leaders were ecstatic, energetic,
and eager to provide running commentary on the
wonders God was performing. Now they were
ready for us pastors. Had we observed the mar-
velous power of God? I was not entirely convinced
of that, but it appeared that most of the contingent
from my town were.

The leader made a few more patronizing comments about us pastors. Then she nailed us to the
wall. "Will all the pastors who want more power for
their ministry please come up here right now," she
cooed.

The earlier decision about standing at her invitation, which angered me at the time, now seemed
innocuous. *Do I want more power for my ministry?*
More power? Me? What for? I'm the powerfullest dude in
three counties. I can't possibly use more power, I said to
me sardonically.

Me dialogued back. *Don't be a fool. You're here with*
well-meaning Christians who love you. You can go along
with this.

I answered myself. *But this is patent manipulation!*
Can truth come out of fraud? Can darkness produce light?
Can deceptive death produce resurrection power?

All right, I said. *Let's drop this silly dialogue.* I bowed
my inner self before God, ashamed that I had been
out of the trusting-Christ mode all evening. I relaxed. God's peace came upon me.

"What shall I do, Lord?" I asked without words. I
waited. This whole thought process had been in-

stantaneous. Now I was in no hurry. The peace of God which passes all understanding overshadowed me.

I began to smile inwardly, aware that once again I had been trapped into taking myself too seriously instead of simply enjoying the Lord Jesus. Quiet love for him came over me right then. I couldn't thank him enough.

I was still listening, but God was yet silent. "O.K., Lord. I'm going up there. But you know I won't keel over just to go along with the crowd. I'm not going to resist either. I'll just trust you and see what happens."

By the time we pastors were lined up across the stage my interior smile had become an outward grin. This would be fun. I was near the end of the line. I had counted about thirty pastors as we walked across in front of the stage, doubling back up the steps at the side.

By the time my end of the line had stopped they had begun praying for those who had arrived first. They had spaced us out shoulder to shoulder, so I couldn't see very well what was happening at the other end of the line. It appeared that man by man they were slumping back into the arms of the catchers.

As they neared me I coached myself. *For sure I'm not planning to fall, but I won't resist.* They were praying for the one next to me. They were praying for me. I experienced limpness, peace, and a sense of melting and slumped into the arms of a huge man standing behind me, who eased me to the floor.

There I lay in wonder, in complete quietness of

body, mind, and spirit. And I was amused. "What can this mean, Lord?" would have been my question had I needed to verbalize.

Back to Jack's Miracle Man

I had walked once around the block. In that brief time several years' worth of skepticism were trying to focus into questions, questions about manipulation, healing, miracles, faith, the power of God in the lives of men and women. *At least,* I thought, *this is a chance to get an up-close investigation of one who claims such a healing. Gene Harbison, here I come!*

SO FAR . . .

- We wonder whether contemporary "miracles" of healing are genuine or fraudulent.
- We feel concern for the spiritual and psychological well-being of persons who express faith for healing but experience no apparent results.
- We feel ambivalence about some popular techniques used in mass meetings by practitioners of the ministry of healing.
- We acknowledge that the biblical record clearly shows that Jesus healed and advocated that his followers offer healing to suffering people.
- We learn of a man who thinks he's been healed of multiple sclerosis.
- We observe a charismatic rally in which the participants believe the power of God is producing miracles.

For Reflection and Discussion

1. In the Introduction the author lists a variety of opinions about miracles. Which one best fits your concept? Try stating your own definition of *miracle*.

2. Do you think it could make a physical difference in the life of a distraught person with high blood pressure to enter a deeper trust and obedience relationship with Jesus Christ? If his or her blood pressure went down, would that constitute a miraculous healing? If you think that would be healing by faith in Christ, is that the same as a miracle?

3. Have you seen religious presentations on TV or at religious rallies in which there seemed to be manipulation? Has anyone tried to manipulate you in your family? at school? at work? in your church?

4. Jesus preached, taught, and healed. He instructed his disciples to do the same. According to episodes in the Book of Acts and James 5:14-16, the early church also practiced the ministry of healing. Tell why you believe there should, or should not, be transference and continuation of this biblical activity to the twentieth-century church.

5. What arguments would you use to dissuade someone who wanted to begin an intentional ministry of healing in your church? Or what arguments would you use to persuade the decision-makers in your church that an intentional ministry of healing is valid?

CHAPTER 2

Human Suffering and the Cross

The Power of the Cross

Fifty or sixty men scuffed and conversed their way into the dimly lit chapel. The room was undistinguished except for its dinginess—and the crucifix, of course, which was obtrusively large for this small room. From it hung the Lord's body wrenched in bleeding agony.

Our red-vested miracle man was one of three leaders seated in the chancel. I sat in the last pew, again not thirty feet from exhibit A. All the men had settled in. Movement stopped. The room was hushed and still as we waited for the opening service to begin. Slowly, distinctly, soundlessly came the thought, *I'm going to teach you something about the cross.*

The meeting began informally with a prayer, a welcome, and an expression of hope that we would be well rewarded for giving up our normal weekend freedom.

Then Gene Harbison introduced Father Tom Henseler, the spiritual director for the Peoria Diocese, who was to give the opening homily. Father Tom was tall and rangy with straight black hair combed back loosely. He was not dressed in clerics. He wore dark slacks and a short-sleeved white sport shirt. The shirt, open at the collar and overhanging his belt line, had several large pastel flowers embroidered on it. He moved easily and spoke quietly. The effect was one of informality and openness. I expected to remain at ease, arms stretched out along the pew back, relaxed physically and only halfway listening to whatever the man might say.

Within seconds after he began his homily, a stirring of energy and interest moved me to mental alertness. I felt as if I should be seated on the front edge of the pew straining forward. Undergirding the simplicity of his words and demeanor came a communion with us listeners, a sense of wonder, of mystery.

He told us about an ancient hymn of the early church. The song tells the story of the Son of God, established with his Father in the richness of love and glory. The Son left the Father's bosom for life on earth, accepting the tawdriness of poverty and assuming the burden of human limitation, except that he lived and loved without sin.

For this sinlessness he was judged by men and women and accepted by God to die by Roman crucifixion. Raw holes were ripped in the tender flesh of hands and feet by dull iron spikes. One massive hammer stroke at a time, the jagged spikes were forced through skin, tissue, blood, and bone into a wooden cross. His broken body drooped in agony from these nails. Hostile onlookers made him the subject of jeers and catcalls as he hung in loneliness, ignominy, public shame, and pain.

Hours later came the sweet release of spirit and body into the unconscious rest of death. Sin hounded him to the cross, nailed him there, and left him dead. The wages of sin is death. Jesus Christ, the unique Son of God, accepted that death of sin in his own body on behalf of humankind. Rather than defeat him, however, sin and its consequences have been killed; for the resurrection power of God brought Jesus alive again from the dead. We know, then, that God, not sin, reigns; we too can sing the ancient hymn in contemporary form, "He is Lord!"

Father Tom explained that the purpose of our weekend together was to regain perspective, to re-instate the event of the death and resurrection of Jesus Christ to its proper place as *the* preeminent fact of our historic faith, rather than one among many.

He pointed out that childhood learning experiences cause many of us to rank various elements of our religious life of equal value, so that we fail properly to distinguish between the more and less important among those daily realities that comprise our patterns of religiosity. Things so disparate as honoring Mother Mary, lighting votive candles, fasting, confession, bingo, and church raffles vie for equal position with the mass, which so powerfully represents the atoning work of Jesus Christ.

Human Suffering

When Father Tom pictured Jesus dragging the heavy cross up the hill to Golgotha, I remembered a

talk I had had with Steve Downey. At age fifteen
Steve was lithe, agile, graceful as the deer he hunted
with bow and arrow in the wooded hills near his
farm home. Like his father and older brothers, he
would be tall and athletic. Already he measured six
feet. The high school basketball coach expected him
to be a star player his sophomore year.

But severe pain in his right hip joint slowed him
down. By Thanksgiving he was hospitalized with
bone cancer rather than cavorting on the basketball
court. I was in my second year as a student pastor
serving the Pine Bluff Methodist Church, to which
the Downeys belonged. Each weekend that winter I
visited Steve at his home or at a nearby hospital.

One bitterly cold day in February I drove to Iowa
City to see Steve, who had been transferred to University Hospital a few weeks earlier. On my previous visit he had been in a room with another teen-
aged boy. This time I was informed that he had been
moved to a ward at the end of the wing. Even before
I reached the double doors to this ward I could hear
muffled screams. Someone was screaming with
pain. *Steve will never be able to rest in there,* I thought.

The ward was one large room with sixteen beds,
eight headed toward each of the outside walls. Each
bed area could be isolated from the others by closing
curtains attached to iron rods with metal fasteners.
Two or three of the patients were secluded in this
way from the mostly open ward. I walked slowly
along the center aisle looking for Steve, thankful the
screams had stopped. The patients were unusually
subdued, no doubt out of empathy with the one
who had been hurting so intensely.

Steve was nowhere to be seen. I was about to

return to the nurses' station for better instructions when I realized he could be in one of the closed-off sections.

The first one I checked proved to be the one. His mother and father were standing at the foot of the bed. A doctor and a nurse stood on one side, two interns on the other. Steve was holding a pillow against his face. "All right, Steve. We're going to leave now," said the doctor. "But we'll be back. We've just got to get some fluids in you." I realized it had been Steve's screams I had heard.

Steve's father motioned me to be seated in one of the metal folding chairs inside the curtain. He and Mrs. Downey sat in two others across the bed from me. Steve remained motionless behind his pillow. For a long time no one spoke. Then his father said quietly, "The reverend's here, Steve." Still no movement. Steve's weight was below eighty pounds. His veins had collapsed. The doctors had been working without success to insert IV needles in new places.

Minutes later Steve lifted one edge of the pillow and spoke to me as evenly as his weakness would allow. "Why is it that every night I pray, and every day I have this same pain?"

I was sadly innocent of both theology and methods of pastoral care. I had no idea what the answer to that question might be. I didn't know an answer and had no plan to say anything. But I wanted to be closer to Steve, so I went over, sat on the edge of the bed, and twisted around with my head down beside his.

Thinking about Jesus, I took Steve's hand in mine. Without planning it, I began to talk quietly. "Steve, do you believe God loved Jesus?" He nodded slightly. "Do you remember how they whipped Jesus, laid a heavy cross on his back, and made him carry it up the hill for his own crucifixion?" I was picturing it in my mind as I talked. "People spat on him. Called him names. Threw stones at him." I had no idea where I was going with this line of thought.

Suddenly I was aware of the scars and bruises on the back of Steve's hands where IV needles had been pulled in and out so many times over the last few months. I had seen similar marks on the top of his feet where the doctors had been working a few minutes earlier to insert the needle for intravenous fluids. The nail marks were there for me. I knew very little theology, but I knew Jesus suffered; and I knew God loved Jesus. "I don't know why you hurt so bad, Steve. But I know God loves you deeply right now." I hadn't said very much. Steve had said nothing since his opening question.

He put the pillow aside and spoke to his father. "Tell the doctors they can come back now," he said. "I'm ready."

Perhaps they were even then on the way. They arrived in very short time. I put my head close to Steve's. He reached one thin arm around it and clasped his hands together. He squeezed my head in his arm as tightly as he could while they worked over his feet. The greater the pain, the greater the pressure he put on my head. But he did not utter a sound.

Minutes later the doctor spoke. "Way to go, Steve," he said, and walked off without further comment. The nurse quickly finished cleaning up, kissed Steve on the forehead, and followed the doctor out of the ward.

Inside I was asking the question again the hundredth time for Steve and—by this juncture in my ministry—a host of other praying sufferers. "Why did he pray every night, and every day suffer that same pain?" Just as the non-answer came that day on his hospital bed in terms of the cross of Christ, so, beneath this looming crucifix, the story of the suffering of God's Son was again being interwoven by word and Spirit with the suffering of all of God's people.

Father Tom had finished his talk. I started to check the time and remembered that they had confiscated our watches for the weekend. We were to be relieved of clock watching, guided from event to event on the unpublished agenda by our leaders. Furthermore, the hours after the final evening session and prior to worship the next morning were to be spent in Benedictine silence. Finding time to question Gene Harbison, it appeared, would be a larger problem than I had anticipated.

One of the leaders stood to conclude this session. He reminded us that following his benediction we were committed to silence until Matins. He prayed. Contrary to the noise of entry, the men moved slowly and quietly from the chapel. I sat absorbed in the death of Jesus and the suffering of humanity.

The Absence of God

Suddenly I remembered a scene from Richard E. Kim's novel, *The Martyred*. "Your god—is he aware of the suffering of his people?" That line came to mind with nearly the impact of the earlier thought, *I'm going to teach you something about the cross.* It was a

question asked of a Christian minister by a propa-
ganda officer in the South Korean army. Although
he was an agnostic, Captain Lee's job was to pro-
pagandize the communist atrocities of the North
Koreans in contrast to the Christian values in the
South.

Lee traveled with Mr. Shin, the minister, to a
bombed-out church. Shin led a fellow minister out
of the charred and dusty rubble by the hand. While
a pastor in North Korea, the man had been bru-
talized by the communist regime. He had escaped
to Seoul, but the devastation of his soul had driven
him insane. Now, hollow-eyed, gaunt, and jaun-
diced, the catatonic pastor shuffled along slowly
beside Shin, who had found him seeking solace
among the ruins of the empty church.

As the two emerged from the dark cavern of
skewed timbers and fallen bricks, Lee remembered
his own angry rampage at a similar cave when he
had been on active duty. The contingent of men he
had been leading found a place in a hillside where
scores of men, women, and children had been
herded into a cave that was then closed by dyna-
mite. They had dug through the dirt and rocks to
find piles of rotting bodies. Among them there were
a few survivors, one of whom Lee had carried out of
the cave.

Captain Lee had knelt over him. He had tried to
comfort the dying man. A news team, cameras
flashing, had hovered around them. One of the
cameramen had asked him to lean back so he could
get a shot of the man. In a rage Lee leaped to his feet,
grabbed a shovel, and began slashing at the cameras.

Lee returned the ministers to their house and turned to leave. Then he spun around. He stood for a moment facing Shin in silence. "Your god—is he aware of the suffering of his people?"

I had used that story a few years earlier as the introduction to a sermon on suffering. "Is God aware of our suffering?" Of course, God is aware—and cares deeply. God loved and cared enough to send Jesus to do something about our sin and suffering.

One Decisive Miracle

Eventually, I followed Jack to our room on the second floor, got ready for bed, and stretched out on the cot. Sleep was far from me. I could hear Jack breathing in slow and easy rhythm. I tried relaxation meditation, just being still and listening for the voice of God to tell me the lesson about the cross. Nothing.

I decided to get dressed and find the prayer room they said would always be open to us. It was a small room on the first floor, the only carpeted room in the building. To my surprise there was quiet conversation in the little room. Two men, kneeling at the altar, were consulting and praying together. There were no chairs. I sat near the back wall so I could lean against it and focus on the worship center, which was comprised of a wooden crucifix and an open Bible flanked by burning candles. Within minutes the men rose, hugged, and one of them left.

The one who remained seated himself on the floor facing the altar. It was Gene Harbison. While I was trying to decide how to break the Benedictine silence without breaking the rules, Gene turned and introduced himself. He explained that team members were scheduled to be available in the prayer room should any of the retreatants desire counseling.

I nodded in understanding and said "thanks" with a tone of dismissal to satisfy him that I was there only for meditation. Seconds later I leaned forward, "May I ask you a question?"

"Sure," he said.

"I overheard someone say you've experienced a miraculous healing. Is that right?"

"Yes."

"Would you mind telling me about it?"

He scooted his way back to lean beside me against the wall and told me this story. By the time he was thirty years old he had worked himself up to ownership of a supermarket. Besides being a workaholic, he lived life in the fast lane. His constantly on-the-move lifestyle put tremendous strain on his family, which consisted of his wife, Ara Ann, and four small children.

He began feeling extreme fatigue. Only with great effort could he force himself out of bed and off to work in the mornings. His work and play schedule was so unrealistic, however, that at first he assumed he was just "burned out" and needed more rest. However, he also found himself losing his balance at times.

Finally, he went to his doctor, who ran preliminary tests and prescribed rest. But Gene got worse. The doctor, suspecting multiple sclerosis, sent Gene to the Mayo Clinic in Rochester for further tests. The preliminary diagnosis was confirmed. The doctors began trying to find ways to help him cope with this disease, for which they said there was no known cure.

As the months went by, Gene's movements became increasingly restricted. He was forced to walk with a cane. He couldn't drive because of double vision. He worked very little. Expenses mounted. Without his supervision, the business waned, and eventually he lost it. His income and health were gone. Life was at a very low ebb for the Harbisons.

The family belonged to the Catholic church. They did not know what to expect from that quarter. Some friends, however, were finding their lives powerfully changed by increased trust in Christ, which they had begun to experience through a retreat movement called Cursillo. They urged Gene and Ara Ann to make a Cursillo at the earliest opportunity.

On the last day of the Cursillo, instead of going to dinner, Gene went to his cot to rest. Two college students, brothers from the University of Illinois who were also making their Cursillo, knew about Gene's plight and decided to pray for his healing.

Together they walked into his room, one carrying a huge black Bible, and both dressed in bib overalls, the college uniform of the day. "Hi, Gene," one said. "God is faithful to his promises. Do you believe that?"

"Yes," he answered.

"Listen to this," said the one with the Bible. "'He himself bore our sins in his body on the tree, so that we might die to sins and live for righteousness; by his wounds you have been healed'" (1 Pet. 2:24). Gene lay there while the student flipped pages to other places in the Bible.

"This is what Jesus says," he continued. "'If two of you shall agree on earth as touching any thing . . . it shall be done for them of my Father which is in heaven' (Matt. 18:19, kjv). Do you mind if we pray for you?"

One of the brothers placed his hand on Gene's right knee and said, "Make this man well; make him whole, in the name of Jesus Christ." A heat sensation started about an inch from Gene's right ankle and went up through the right side of his body and over his shoulder. The other brother placed his hand on Gene's left knee. The same heat sensation came up the left side of his body, across the chest area, up through the inside of his throat, behind the left eye, inside his skull, over his right eye, and then out of the middle of his forehead.

"I tell you," Gene said, "when you feel the heat sensation and the pain leaves and the feeling is back in your legs and hands and your eyesight's back, all you can do is say, 'Thank God!'"

He was sitting on an army cot. He remembered the brothers leaving. He lay back in peace. The presence of the Lord was no more than six or eight inches from his right hand.

Gene continued his story. "Again I didn't know what to say. It was kind of frightening. I said, 'Thank you.' And the response was, 'Gene, get up off that cot; you're fine.' Not in an audible voice, as you and I have been talking, but in a Divine Presence."

Gene lay quietly for a few moments in awe and wonder. Then he sat up on the edge of the bed. He tried to stand and found it was no problem. He took a few balanced steps. No problem. He realized he was moving normally. He walked into the dining room where the men were occupied with food and conversation. When his friends saw him enter unaided by cane or human help, they were stunned. They were witnessing a miracle while some thirty other men talked, laughed, and ate.

One of the highlights of Cursillo is the Closura. After the retreatants have been separated from family and business routine for seventy-two hours, friends and family are invited to observe the lengthy closing session. This consists of a time of praise and thanksgiving and an opportunity for the participants to say publicly what the retreat experience has meant to them.

The testimonies were thrilling. The men were excited. But the meeting was two hours old, and Ara Ann was eager to get Gene home again. Besides, she knew he was self-conscious about the crippled gait with which he moved. She doubted he would cane his way to the mike even if he had experienced God's presence in a new dimension, as so many other claimed.

And then she saw him stand and slide the chair away. Watching in love, she expected to see him hobble courageously to center floor.

Instead, he moved fluidly, gracefully. He had no cane. For the first time in years she saw her husband walk without a cane or without leaning on someone's arm. Ara Ann burst into tears as Gene told how Christ's death on the cross had been applied to his life by the prayer of faith; how the healing power from the wounds of Christ flowed through his body; how the presence of the Lord Jesus had appeared by his cot; and how he had stood to walk in freedom and wonder. That night Gene drove the car home for the first time in years.

I sat there just as stunned by his story as if I had been at the Cursillo two years earlier when it happened. I had heard about miracles but had always thought there would be a better explanation if only I could know all the facts. This time I was close enough to be convinced.

Gene's replacement came, and he left for bed. I continued, awestruck, to lean against the wall for a long time. I thanked the Lord God Almighty for the power of the cross. "By his wounds you have been healed!" Now those words were more than a verse. They were a matter of incontrovertible experience. Gene Harbison had been miraculously healed.

But Steve Downey, tall, lithe, and graceful, at age sixteen . . . died.

The Causes of Sin and Suffering

The crucifixion of Jesus Christ shows God has done the utmost to alleviate sin and suffering ("He who did not spare his own Son, but gave him up for us all—how will he not also . . . graciously give us all things," Rom. 8:32). Why, then, does it so often seem God is deaf to our prayers and absent from our cause? Let us consider three biblical explanations for sin and suffering, assuming the background of the Lord's untainted creation.

The totally "good" (Gen. 1:26-31) plan of the Creator for human well-being was for us to live in trusting, obedient fellowship with God. The world would be a sin-free paradise without suffering or disease. But human disobedience aborted this plan.

Since the Fall, human well-being continues to be subject to the imperfect functioning of a natural order cursed by God (Gen. 2:16-17; 3:6-8, 17-19) and given over to the interim control of "the powers of darkness." Just as thorns, thistles, death, and dust (Gen. 3:17-19) entered into what had been God's good creation, so also did disease, like cancer; geophysical upheavals, like earthquakes; and atmospheric tragedies, like tornadoes, none of which were a part of God's original "good" creation.

A second cause of spiritual, emotional, and physical ill health is exemplified by a child born into a home where he or she cannot experience love. A variety of inappropriate emotional warpings may occur that can be attributed to lack of love in the family. If we determine the fault to be with the parents and seek to analyze their failure, we may be pushed back a second generation to the grandparents' unloving household. Sometimes it appears we are committed to an infinite regress. Exodus 20:4-6 states that the sins of the fathers who refuse to worship and serve the Lord are visited on their progeny for several generations. Thus, it is common to see a need for what is today often termed "healing of the memories" in persons whose emotional maladjustments precipitate illnesses of various kinds. The antidote to this kind of dis-ease is not merely psychotherapy but more often a spiritual ministry to the inner being.

The third—and most obvious—impediment to total well-being is personal sin. There is much evidence that a life of sin produces ill health. In his letter to the Romans Paul clearly states that those who worship created things rather than the Creator are "given over" to impurity, degradation, and death (1:18-25; 3:9-18, 23). From this the only salvation is the redemptive plan of God through the healing love of Jesus Christ, the Son.

The Fall left humankind in desperate need. Three terrible malady-producing factors worked in interrelated conspiracy to comprise this need: a disease-prone universe; the "sins of the fathers" causing adverse emotional conditions in children through several generations; and the more direct ill effects of human sin.

Humanity's struggle to survive against such overwhelming malevolence produces only fragmentation, distortion, suffering, and death. A power greater than humanity is required if we are to overcome. That power is made available through the redemptive intervention of an alternate plan for cohesive well-being in fellowship with the Creator. It is a plan to restore humanity to proper communion with God, good relationships with other human beings, and harmonious functioning of body, mind, and spirit in individual lives. It is a plan motivated by divine love, accomplished by the redemptive mission of Jesus Christ (John 3:16), and ministered by God's grace through faith (Eph. 2:8-9).

SO FAR . . .

• We are deeply burdened with the magnitude of human suffering.

- We are humbled with the knowledge that God's Son was crucified for the sins of humanity.
- We struggle with the knowledge that not all who believe are physically healed.
- We identify three biblical causes for sin and suffering: the Fall and its consequent evils; adverse family patterns which pass on brokenness from generation to generation; and the devastating ill effects of personal and corporate sin.
- We come to believe experientially as well as theoretically that healing miracles occur.
- We learn that Christ's death on the cross provides power through which faith accomplishes healing in human life.

For Reflection and Discussion

1. St. Paul anchors his theology in the crucifixion of Jesus Christ (e.g., 1 Cor. 2:1-5). What advantage or disadvantage does such a biblical theology have for understanding the ministry of healing?

2. Most of us have experienced at times a sense of sadness and inadequacy when faced with the knowledge of terminal illness in someone close to us. What have you found to be helpful in relating to such a person or his/her family?

3. One of the arguments against the existence of God is God's apparent absence in dealing with the huge amount of suffering in the world. What biblical and experiential evidence can you cite for the involvement of God in contemporary human history?

4. The author acknowledges being decisively influenced

by hearing firsthand the story of a man healed of multiple sclerosis. Can you think of an explanation for this miracle other than an act of God? Can you tell of any miracle healing which you believe was accomplished by divine intervention?

5. The author lists three biblical explanations for human suffering. Can you think of others? Which of the three do you believe is the greatest cause of human suffering?

CHAPTER 3

The Difference
Faith Makes

The Need for Reevaluation

The Gene Harbison story stunned me. Intellectual pride had caused me to discount most of what happened at the charismatic healing rally. It seemed to be a kind of cheerleading that psyched people up to feel better, perhaps only temporarily. Now I was forced to reevaluate my experiences with "healers" in the light of the Harbison miracle.

Marjorie's "Psychosomatic" Arthritis Healed

I had wistfully dismissed two other cases of obvious physical healing as merely psychosomatic. Marjorie Stone taught grammar school in the little town where I had been the United Methodist pastor five years earlier. She was a quiet lady, gentle and effective with the children. Although Marjorie was an active church member, I was unaware that she suffered terrible arthritic pain most of the time.

A group of nine persons from the church committed ourselves to a thirty-day program called the John Wesley Great Experiment. The plan was to follow a defined set of spiritual disciplines for one month, meeting together weekly for prayer and evaluation, to "experiment" with the results in our lives. An important part of the discipline was a series of directed steps for morning prayer to be carried out each day from 5:30 to 6:00 A.M.

It was Thursday evening, the third week of the program. The meeting was almost over before she said anything, which was typical of Marjorie.

"My arthritis is gone," she said, her voice barely audible. There was a wonderful glow about her, but I didn't understand the significance of her words. Actually, I wasn't sure I had heard her clearly. No one responded, so she said it again, this time with a touch more clarity and emphasis. "My arthritis is gone!"

When she finally got our attention, this is what she told us. Her arthritis had become increasingly painful, so she went to the doctor Tuesday afternoon. He doubled the dosage level for her pain medicine. The next morning during prayer time the Holy Spirit led her to face and deal with a series of resentments. She forgave the persons involved and asked the Lord Jesus to forgive her for her unChristlike attitude.

By noon she realized all the stiffness had gone out of the problem joints, so she didn't take the pain medicine. She never needed it again.

I began to consider an alternative to my psycho-somatic explanation for Marjorie's case. This was not merely a minor reordering of the psyche. This was a *spiritual* matter. This was an encounter with the God of our salvation, who through Jesus Christ provided the essential healing.

What Marjorie experienced was conviction of sin by the pinpoint revelation of the Holy Spirit, heart-felt repentance for her offense against God and humanity, and a powerful inner cleansing through the atoning work of Jesus Christ. It was this divine intervention which left her free from sin and arthritic bondage to pain.

No psychotherapist, apart from the grace of God, could have brought her to so redemptive a cure. Here was an experience (though the Lord certainly addressed her through the psyche) that began with the spirit, proceeded through the emotions, and culminated in the physical: spirit, mind, and body. Was not this just as much a healing as that experienced by Gene Harbison?

Why, then, had I been too obtuse to recognize it as a miracle at the time? Had I been so conditioned by the world view of western civilization that my mind refused to stretch around the idea of miracles? Or did I simply hold to too narrow a definition for divine healing?

During the next few weeks I began to reconsider a number of previous experiences in the light of the cross. Though my belief was still naive and un-taught, I had no doubt that Christ had been actively healing in situations where I had failed to recognize him and give him the credit.

Depression, Asthma, and High Blood Pressure Healed?

No case was more blatant than my own, in which physical and emotional healings were obvious, though not instantaneously complete. More to the point, they were so distinctly secondary to my experience as a new creation in Christ that I barely acknowledged them. For some reason I had never thought of myself as having been healed. Now I was revising that opinion.

Introspection was the name of my game. From childhood until just before my thirty-third birthday I spent most of my time—whatever else I appeared to be doing, working, playing basketball or softball, writing, being with the family—thinking about myself.

I was mentally cut off from the emotional springs of my thought and behavior. Irrational decisions were commonplace. Normal family relationships with both my parents and my wife and children were impossible because of my unpredictability.

During these years, though I job-hopped from banking to teaching to social work to the bowling business, I considered myself a writer. I worked at various tent-making jobs while thinking about being a writer, attending writers' schools and conferences, meeting with writers' groups, and on rare occasions, actually writing something. It was a life ideally suited to producing misery. In my mind this melancholia substantiated the writer's calling. The one who suffers is qualified to reproduce literary life without superficial mendacity.

THE DIFFERENCE FAITH MAKES

What it produced was high-grade mental illness in the form of chronic depression. In addition, my susceptibility to asthma attacks was so brittle that I spent weeks of nonsleep agony every allergenic season struggling for oxygen. These were years of sporadic psychotherapy, including thirteen electroshock therapy treatments and constant strong dosages of antidepressant drugs. I took additional medication for my allergies and made frequent appearances at the hospital emergency room for adrenalin shots and/or oxygen. For me—for us—life was anything but fun.

I had one more malady which is easily documented and no surprise—high blood pressure. After purchasing a small bowling business, I felt I needed to obtain a term life insurance policy. The cost turned out to be prohibitive because of the high rating due to the blood pressure readings discovered during my physical exam for the policy.

Chronic depression, asthma, high blood pressure, and intolerably poor family relationships kept me in constant despair. I did not want to spend any more years in this condition.

One midnight at closing time I locked myself inside rather than outside the Topspot Bowling Lanes. I thought I had tried everything in search of meaning except God. (Actually, I had tried that, too, but I hadn't known how to make it more than a head trip.) I decided to try to find God's way as a last resort.

I don't know if there is a God or not, I thought. *But if there is, and God makes himself known to me, I know that I ought to live differently than I am.* I did not anticipate any experienced revelation. I simply meant to find some way of ascertaining whether what I had picked up about God along the way was valid.

At the same time I was thinking, *If God doesn't make himself known to me, it doesn't make any difference whether there's a God or not.* I had no idea how biblically sound this line of reasoning was. Later I would learn that we can never find God by our own efforts; that God was revealed through Jesus Christ and continues to become known through the word and church by the activity of the Holy Spirit.

I had failed during my years in and around the church to appropriate any significant information about the life, death, and resurrection of God's Son, Jesus Christ. What I had to act on was merely a vague sense that going God's way meant revising my moral standards; that is, to stop doing what I knew to be "wrong" and begin doing those things I knew to be "right." This would give me plenty to work on.

Armed with this line of reasoning, I walked to a scorer's table and sat down. I tore a score sheet off the pad, turned it over and made two lists, one of activities that must stop and one of those things I must do. *From now on,* I thought with determination, *I'm going to live this way.* I had formulated the plan. All that remained was to follow the plan and put "God's way" to the test. I crumpled up the score sheet, threw it on the floor, and left.

Late the next morning I arrived to prepare for the noon opening. The Topspot was a small ten-lane place with only one full-time employee other than myself and some part-timers. My management style was for each of us to do some of everything. It was my day to sweep up the approaches and dress the alleys. As I pushed the wide dust mop ahead of me, that crumpled score sheet with my revised life plan written on it slid along lightly with a small amount of lint, dust, and other debris. I knew exactly what was listed there. I anticipated no problems and no revelations.

I can't recall now what was on those lists, except for three minor bad habits which I planned to abandon—cigar smoking, using gutter language, and bowling in pot games for stakes I couldn't afford.

The usual afternoon crowd began to gather. Alley men who worked evenings, a cigarette salesman who interrupted his route most days for a few pot games, a couple of would-be pros who bowled a hundred games a week. They all carried averages ten to thirty pins better than mine, but I loved to bowl with them. It got my mind off my misery. Besides, I always told myself, it was good business for me to get in the game. And I didn't mind winning occasionally.

One by one they changed shoes, made their way to the approaches, and began warming up. Ken started listing names on the score sheet. "Who's in?" he asked.

"Count me out," I said. "I'm going to work on spares." I switched on a lane away from the match and began to loosen up. Smooth, beautifully smooth was my stroke that day. I couldn't leave a spare.

I strolled over to watch the game as the big boys were moving into the tenth frame. Their scores weren't that great. I made a few cute comments. Just slightly off-color. Good for laughs. Someone spit out a raunchy comeback. The repartee got funnier, dirt-

ier. No one was better at it than I. "Pencil me in for
the next game," I said, on my way to the counter for
a cigar. I would start my new life tomorrow.

Every few days I would try again to straighten my
life out, but it never lasted. Weeks stretched into
months without any change. I kept thinking that
this plan had merit, that if only I could live right
things might get better for me. Instead, my despair
got deeper.

One of the things I liked to do for relaxation was to
get out and drive on the highway at night. I had a big
boat of a car, a '59 DeSoto with a great radio. Late one
spring night I was out cruising along, more or less at
peace with myself. The driver's side window was
down. Fresh night air streamed across my face.

I began thinking how easy it should be to follow
that simple list of do's and don'ts. My sickening
inability to live right for even one day disgusted me.
Strangely, my despair seemed minimal. I felt as if I
were part of the night being blown along in the
wind.

Gradually a thought formed inside me. It came
from somewhere beneath or beyond my conscious
mind. It seemed just to appear there, really without
words and without effort. It wasn't exactly an idea.
It was more a feeling, and the feeling was a prayer.

When I tried to verbalize what the prayer said it
was this: "God, I can't do that. If you want me to do
it, you'll have to do it in me." I had no idea what that
meant. I only know that on later reflection I would
say that was the first real prayer I ever offered. And
yet it was not I that prayed. It was the Holy Spirit
praying in me.

No unusual elation occurred. I didn't know at the

time that it was the beginning of an entirely new way of life, a rebirth into the life of God's Spirit. I rode home much at peace with myself, feeling a part of the wind and of the night.

It was the next afternoon at work that I noticed something new about my life. I was getting a pair of rental shoes for a young man who bowled occasionally at the Topspot. He always rubbed me the wrong way. This time he was unhappy with the first pair I offered and asked for different shoes, which I happily provided. How surprised I was to realize there was no irritation for me in this simple transaction. Normally, though I may not have shown it, I would have been disgusted with the guy.

Furthermore, I began to enjoy all the customers. Before that day they had only been an inconvenience for me. Now I saw them as real people. For the first time in my life I was seeing other human beings as valid, worthy of my attention. Heretofore everyone else had been merely extensions of myself. I was my whole world. Whoever else appeared there, including God, had no status. I was my own everything. And it was not enough.

I began to feel great. Vibrant. Alive. Still, I wasn't making a definite connection between this changed attitude and my midnight prayer. That came a few days later.

It was certainly not my custom to read the Bible. Whenever I had tried that in the past, it proved uninteresting. For some reason, however, I found myself reading, "But the fruit of the Spirit is love, joy, peace, patience, kindness, goodness, faithfulness, gentleness, self-control" (Gal. 5:22-23, RSV). I have no idea whether I picked it up and came across this in the midst of a passage or whether I opened it to this place and read only this verse. What I *do* know is that I was amazed. What truth! What reality! *This is the truest thing I've ever read,* I thought.

In a flash, the midnight prayer, the new love for people, the new authority of the Bible, and the knowledge that all this "new" reality was the fruit of the Holy Spirit put life in focus for me. It was a new me. I knew there was a God, for God *had* become known to me. Incredible amounts of working out my own salvation lay ahead, but by the grace of God the new creation had occurred.

I had a new nature. Somewhere in the hidden recesses of my inner being the Holy Spirit of our Lord Jesus had entered into intimate union with my spirit. The new union was tiny, but incontrovertible; small, but powerful.

Although outward manifestations were not obvious at first, inwardly my life plans were being gradually revised; *and* within months there were wonderful improvements in my health. A trip to give blood at the local blood bank revealed that my blood pressure was back to normal. The autumn asthma attacks that year were much less frequent and less severe, and I was at no time forced to cancel an activity because of one. Soon asthma attacks became a thing of the past.

The most prodigious and exhilarating change was my release from chronic depression. Once I battled a constant sense of deadness. Now I was alive! Often vibrantly alive.

There remained seasons of depression but with a thrilling difference. Previously the depression was compounded by despair. I thought I would always feel that way or worse, apart from drugs which produced undesirable side effects. Depression still produced misery, but I knew it was temporary. I lived in hope rather than despair. What a difference faith makes!

Had I been aware then, as I am now, of the Lord's ministry of healing, I would have realized the miraculous quality of these lovely kingdom signs. The healing dimension of my miracle was not as sudden as Gene Harbison's, but it was nonetheless—and continues to be—healing in the deepest sense of the word. I began to think of healing as one part of God's salvation process, a process that would not be complete until we reach wholeness of body, mind, and spirit.

How Jesus Healed

Now that I had begun to reconsider healing as a valid part of God's saving work in the lives of people, I was eager to reread the Gospels from this perspective. Previously, I had somehow been able to filter the healing episodes out of my consideration, to read around and over them as if they were not relevant to twentieth-century Christian life. On this reading they seemed to be at the heart of everything Jesus did.

The healing love of God is clearly expressed in the life and ministry of Jesus Christ. "For God so loved the world," the motive, "that he gave his one and only Son," the method, "that whoever believes in him shall not perish but have eternal life," the goal (John 3:16).

God's goal is for us to have life. "The thief comes

only to steal and kill and destroy; I have come that they may have life, and have it to the full" (John 10:10). Anything that is detrimental to well-being, tending toward death, is a deterrent to the life God desires for us.

That Jesus came to bring life means that his loving purpose includes overcoming those things that interfere with it, such as disease, whether it be physical, emotional, or spiritual. Jesus came to bring salvation, healing, and wholeness.

The translators of the King James Version of the Bible sometimes chose to render *sozo* in English "heal," sometimes "save," and sometimes "made whole" (e.g., Luke 8:36, Mark 5:23, Matt. 9:21-22). They allowed the same variable in *diasozo*. Where it occurs in Luke 7:3, we find "heal." In Matthew 14:36 they say "made perfectly whole."

The evidence of the Gospels is that Jesus' healing ministry was both widespread and overwhelmingly successful. (The one exception is the return to his hometown, Matthew 13:53-58, where the people "took offense" at him, asking, "Isn't this the carpenter's son?" Verse 58 states, "And he did not do many miracles there because of their lack of faith.") Elsewhere we find statements like these taken from the Gospel of Matthew:

> Jesus went throughout Galilee, teaching in their synagogues, preaching the good news of the kingdom, and *healing every disease and sickness among the people*. (4:23)
> When evening came, many who were demon-possessed were brought to him, and he drove out

the spirits with a word and *healed all the sick.* (8:16)

Many followed him, and he *healed all their sick.* (12:15)

People brought all their sick to him and begged him to let the sick just touch the edge of his cloak, and *all who touched him were healed.* (14:36)

Great crowds came to him, bringing *the lame, the blind, the crippled, the dumb and many others,* and laid them at his feet; and *he healed them.* (15:30)

Large crowds followed him, and *he healed them* there. (19:2)

The Centrality of Faith

In addition to this massive number of healings, a few have been selected by the Gospel writers for greater detail. Though the means vary, there is one essential: an activated expression of faith in Jesus for healing. The faith may be expressed by the person who is suffering. Sometimes it is the faith of a relative, a superior, or a friend.

Faith Expressed by the Sufferer

In some cases, initiation of the healing encounter is made by the individual with the problem. A man covered with leprosy saw Jesus in a town one day. The man fell on his face before Jesus and begged him, "Lord, if you are willing, you can make me clean." Jesus responded, "I am willing. Be clean." The leprosy left him immediately (Luke 5:12-14).

In another situation two blind men cried out for his mercy. Jesus took them indoors and asked if they believed. If so, he could restore their sight. "Yes, Lord," they replied. "According to your faith will it be done to you," Jesus said, having touched their eyes, and they were able to see (Matt. 9:27-31).

A third case where initiating faith was evidenced by the diseased person occurred as Jesus was walking along in a group of people on his way to restore a ruler's daughter who had died. A woman in the crowd who had been subject to bleeding touched the edge of his cloak. "Take heart, daughter, your faith has healed you," Jesus said, and she was made well from that moment (Matt. 9:20-22).

Faith Expressed by Another

The healing power of Jesus also proves efficacious in situations where the sick person is not the initiator of the faith encounter. A Canaanite mother whose daughter suffered from demon possession entered into discussion with Jesus and his disciples. She begged him to help her daughter, only to have the disciples urge him to send her away because she was a foreigner. She persisted, saying even dogs eat the crumbs from beneath their masters' tables. Whereupon Jesus responded, "Woman, you have great faith! Your request is granted." The daughter "was healed from that very hour" (Matt. 15:21-28). Presumably the daughter was not even present. We don't know that she lacked faith. We do know that it was a second party who activated the faith in the presence of Jesus, the compassionate healer.

In another case some elders of the Jews came to ask Jesus to assist a centurion who had befriended

Israel by building a synagogue. The centurion, whose servant was ill, had heard of Jesus but considered himself unworthy to come personally to make an appeal for the servant's healing. Jesus agreed to go. The centurion sent friends to intercept Jesus, that he might not have to finish the trip and enter his house. The centurion had sent the message that he understood the authority in chain of command and that Jesus need only "say the word, and my servant will be healed." Amazed, Jesus said to the crowd, "I tell you, I have not found such great faith even in Israel." When the delegation returned, they found the servant healed (Luke 7:1-10).

Another case demonstrating the exercise of faith other than, though possibly in addition to, the suffering person is the story of the paralyzed man carried to Jesus on a mat. Because of the crowd of onlookers, many of them critics from other towns, the mat-bearers could not bring their friend directly to Jesus, so they climbed to the roof with him, removed the tile, and lowered him right in front of Jesus. "When Jesus saw their faith, he said, 'Friend, your sins are forgiven.' " After a theological lesson to the demurring Pharisees and teachers of the law he concluded, "I tell you, get up, take your mat and go home." Whereupon the man rose praising God, and went home (Luke 5:17-26).

These stories demonstrate that healing can come to an ailing person through channels of faith provided by someone else. Resistance from the sufferer could probably prevent the healing; but, at least, it is possible for expressed faith by others to allow the healing love of Jesus access to the problem areas.

No Standard Procedure

We might assume that a careful study of the healing episodes of Jesus would produce some standard pattern or preferred form through which he accomplished his benign purpose. To the contrary, the healing ministry of Jesus reveals about as many different methods as there are stories of healing. Jesus dealt with persons according to their specific needs. He sought to inspire a faith relationship rather than to function out of a formula.

Most of the healing encounters of Jesus involve the use of verbal and/or physical interchange with the person to be healed. The encounter may be verbal only, touch only, or words and touch in combination. On occasion Jesus employs a fourth method, the use of special means, such as saliva or mud.

Verbal Only

In the case mentioned above, which illustrates faith exercised for a friend by those who carried him to Jesus on a mat, there was no use of touch or other physical media (Matt. 9:1-8). Only a verbal affirmation is given. First, "Take heart, son, your sins are forgiven." This was followed by a command from Jesus. "Get up, take your mat and go home."

Another situation where the healings are accomplished through verbal expression only is that of the ten lepers (Luke 17:11-19). In this case the lepers call from a distance, "Jesus, Master, have pity on us!" His response was, "Go, show yourselves to the priests." This was the appropriate action to take for cleansed lepers in order that they might be certified to return to society. They were healed as they went. No touch; merely verbal command.

Touch Only

On other occasions no words are spoken. The mere touch of Jesus accomplished the healing. For example, two blind men called out to Jesus as he and his disciples were leaving Jericho. When he inquired what they wanted they answered, "Lord, we want our sight." Without a word Jesus touched their eyes and they received their sight (Matt. 20:29-34).

Or Matthew 8:14-15: "When Jesus came into Peter's house, he saw Peter's mother-in-law lying in bed with a fever. He touched her hand and the fever left her, and she got up and began to wait on him."

The nonverbal touch from Jesus is enough to allow healing power to flow. Touching Jesus by the diseased person also was effective. This is demonstrated by the poignant story of the woman who had been bleeding for twelve years. She touched the edge of his cloak and was healed. Jesus realized healing power had been tapped by her touch (Luke 8:43-48). Here again, there was healing without words, prayer, or command.

Verbal and Physical

Sometimes verbal and physical means are used in combination. Remember the leper who prostrated himself before Jesus and begged for cleansing. Jesus reached out and touched him, saying at the same time, "I am willing. Be clean!" And the leprosy left him (Luke 5:12-14).

Another case where both verbal and physical forms are used is reported about a crippled woman who for eighteen years had been unable to straighten up at all. Jesus called her to him and announced, "Woman, you are set free from your infirmity." Then he put his hands on her and she straightened up (Luke 13:10-13).

Special Means

In addition to verbal, physical, and word/touch in combination, there are also healing miracles where some other agency is included. In the region of the Decapolis some people brought to Jesus a deaf man who could hardly talk. First Jesus put his fingers into the man's ears. Then he spat and touched the man's tongue. He looked to heaven and said, "Be opened," and the man was able to hear and speak (Mark 7:32-35).

Finally, there is the case of the man blind from birth. Jesus spat on the ground, made some mud, and put it on the eyes of the blind man. He told him to go wash in the pool of Siloam. The man went and washed and came home seeing (John 9:1-11).

The Lesson of Faith

I had known for years that faith in Jesus Christ makes a vital difference in the quality of life people experience. In retrospect, I began to give myself permission to use the term *healing* in this regard. Rereading the Gospels convinced me that the healing miracles of Jesus, always accomplished through faith, were an integral part of his mission to bring salvation, healing, and wholeness to the people of a dying world.

Whatever the method chosen, no matter who provides the primary channel of faith, Jesus is the Great Physician. With compassionate understanding, he applies the most propitious method and achieves benign results. He came out of love (John 3:16) to bring life (John 10:10) to dying humanity. His methods were secondary to his motives. The model he provides for his followers, therefore, is one that clearly elevates vital compassion above doctrine and ritual. The words, the touch, the instructions, the encouragements of various kinds are instructive to the church. But they must always remain secondary to the motivation of life-giving love expressed through a vital trust relationship with Jesus Christ.

SO FAR . . .

- We reconsider the validity of spiritual dynamics and terminology as basic to the cure of psychosomatic maladies.
- We reconsider application of the terms *miracle* and *healing* to cures that are gradual and ongoing as well as instantaneous.
- We find that, out of love, God sent Jesus to bring life (in terms of salvation, healing, and wholeness) to humankind.
- We find no standard procedure for healing in the ministry of Jesus. Instead, there were always compassion and understanding for the need of the person in trouble.
- We see that healing comes from Jesus and is re-

ceived by faith, though not always expressed by
the suffering person.

For Reflection and Discussion

1. Many, if not most, of the people who go to physicians
have psychosomatic illnesses. Can you give instances
that support or dispute such high estimates?
2. The author says, "Jesus came to bring salvation, healing, and wholeness." Give examples showing how this is
happening in your own life or the life of someone about
whom you know.
3. Read Matthew 13:53-58. Notice that Jesus had little
success with healing there, because of the "lack of faith."
On a scale of one to ten (ten being the highest), how
much faith for healing is there in your community? in
your church? in your own relationship to God?
4. The study shown in this chapter concludes that Jesus
used no standard method for healing but related to each
situation with compassion. Are you familiar with healers
or ministries of healing that emphasize one method only?
5. The cases of the Canaanite woman's daughter, the
centurion's servant, and the man carried to Jesus on a mat
are cited as evidence of someone other than the diseased
person expressing faith in Jesus for healing. Can you tell
of a situation where someone was helped through the
faith of another person? Have you ever prayed for someone to be healed?

CHAPTER 4

The Sacramental Model

Introducing the Ministry of Healing to the Church

I was thirty-three years old when faith in Christ became a reality for me and began to change my life. Not long after, I responded to the call to preach and became a student pastor. This work was challenging and rewarding, but it was three churches and many years later before the Gene Harbison encounter crystallized my personal certainty of God's love as an agent of healing. Now I was eager to activate an intentional ministry of healing in our congregation as soon as possible.

Located just off the square in Canton, Illinois, Wesley Church, a fortress-like stone building with massive stained-glass windows, is obviously the most imposing structure around. In our little town she may have been queen of the city's churches.

Being queen of the churches, however, was not for

everyone predicated on being a fortress of the faith. For some, tradition, respectability, and dignity would be more appropriate descriptive words for the church's virtue in the community. Healing services would have been considered strange, if not objectionable. Most members of the congregation were probably unaware that healings even took place (although such stories occasionally appeared in sermon illustrations), let alone received endorsement from their pastor.

The Charismatic Factor

But there were a few who knew otherwise. Remember the carload of revelers who took me to the charismatic rally? And people like Jan, for example, who had once come to my study all aflutter with exciting news. She had been baptized in the Holy Spirit. We rejoiced together over her new-found enthusiasm for God and her gift of speaking in tongues.

I didn't tell her about my own discovery of the gift of tongues during my student days at Garrett Evangelical Theological Seminary. That was in 1962, when the charismatic movement was just getting a foothold in some of the mainline churches. One of the men in my preaching class received an invitation from a friend in Wilmette for the class to attend a healing service at an Episcopal church.

The invitation was surprisingly detailed. It prescribed that everyone who attended should commit themselves to prior study of Acts 2, Romans 12, Ephesians 4, and First Corinthians 12-14. Three of us from the class accepted the invitation and joined the sophisticated lady from the North Shore for the long drive to attend the meeting.

It lasted an amazing four hours. First we gathered in the fellowship hall, listened to a forty-five-minute tape on healing, and spent another fifteen minutes or so updating long lists of prayer requests that the in-house people carried in notebooks.

Then we moved to the nave, where a large group of worshipers were gathering for the service. Two Episcopal priests led the celebration of the Eucharist. Participants were then invited to kneel at the communion rail for anointing, laying on of hands, and prayers for healing by the clergy.

By this time it was 10:30, a reasonable time to depart. Not so, as we had been warned in the invitation. Those who wished to stay returned to the fellowship hall for coffee, conversation, and more cigarette smoke than I had ever seen in a church.

The *big* event, we had been told, was saved for last—and only for the favored few. After the crowd had thinned out, the in-group went to a room upstairs. A circle of about forty chairs had been placed in the center of the room.

Someone with a guitar led us in singing choruses. I felt uncomfortable, since the words for the songs were not provided. Before long the songs were interspersed with prayers from one or another of those around the circle, or an admonition of some kind, or a pronouncement about what we might expect from God.

Then someone uttered a long series of what seemed to me to be nonsense syllables. I was reminded of Ella Fitzgerald, a favorite jazz singer of mine, doing a scat chorus or improvising a be-bop phrase on an old standard tune.

A hush of anticipation came over the group. Another person, speaking in firm, dramatic tones, announced something that sounded like a paragraph from the Old Testament. In King James English, its words seemed repetitive to me. Finally, he said, "I, the Lord, have spoken."

Everyone seemed awestruck by this visitation from on high. I was not so sure. Maybe I was feeling guilty because I had not thought it necessary to submit to the requirement of rereading those scripture passages, so I didn't know the biblical background. Maybe I was just uncomfortable being in a situation that was foreign to my cultural religious experience.

More singing and ecstatic utterances followed. Then one of the priests gave a brief explanation of the baptism in the Holy Spirit. From his approach I assumed there were other neophytes in the circle besides us seminarians. At any rate, the invitation was that members of the group were available to pray with those who wished to receive the gift.

I can't recall whether I requested it or not, but two people drew up chairs in front of me to talk over my needs. Since I was scheduled for my first preaching mission ever in a few weeks, that was uppermost in my mind as a prayer concern. They seemed disappointed that I didn't recognize my deeper need. I noticed that they took my hands to pray for me rather than laying hands on my head as they had been doing for others.

The dorm was quiet when I returned. Few students were around for the summer. There was no roommate to disturb my thoughts and evening prayer time.

Nevertheless, I passed up my usual time of Bible reading and prayer at my desk. I slipped into bed thinking I would pray there and drop off to sleep. Events of the evening were replayed under the light of editorial opinion from my store of preconceptions.

For me, the term *charismatic Christian* was redundant. My preferred definition of Christian at the time was "one in whom the Spirit of Christ dwells." Charismatic means "grace gifted." I knew myself to be both indwelt by the Holy Spirit and gifted. What were these people saying that was different?

A holy light of perspective gradually dawned on me as I prayed. These people were not perfect, but they were urgently seeking God's way. Could I do more? I had seated myself on the judge's bench long before we arrived in that room.

Our friend from Wilmette turned me off from the moment I got into the car. Her series of shallow comments revealed a combination of spiritual immaturity and pride. But what qualified me to be her judge? I knew nothing of the forces that shaped her life and with which she battled.

I turned from judging, gave thanks for exposure to the wonderful "new" way God was working through the priests, and began to sing quiet songs of praise. Soon I ran out of known words, but I went right on singing in sounds that to me had the meaning of praise. Speaking in tongues? *I can do that,* I

thought; so I continued praying in that unedited
flow of sounds that brings so great a sense of release.
I was a tongues-speaking charismatic!

For me it was a private, personal matter. Never
have I felt led to speak publicly, though I have attended large charismatic services where we all sang
in the Spirit. Bill Thomas, who pastored the huge
First United Methodist Church in Tulsa, told of
teaching a year-long course on the Holy Spirit to
hundreds of students. At the end of the year he
asked class members to raise their hand if they
thought he exercised the gift of tongues. About half
thought he did, and the other half thought he
didn't. "Good," he said. "That's just the way I want
it. Only my wife and the Lord know." I really didn't
care whether people knew it or not. For me it was an
insignificant matter.

However, some of the charismatics at Wesley
Church found it strange that I could affirm them in
their new gift without urging the rest of the congregation to the same exhilarating experience. Several
of them made their way to the Assembly of God
church, which was experiencing rejuvenation at the
time.

I missed Mark and Alice most. We had been
through deep struggles together over the life problems the Lord was working out between them. I
loved them. Mark came to his last hopeful interview
with me armed with a worn pamphlet he had
picked up at a Full Gospel Businessmen's rally.

"Did you know," he asked, finger inserted at the
proper place in his booklet, "that John Wesley spoke
in tongues?"

"I didn't know that, Mark," I said, "but it

wouldn't surprise me." I had read much of Wesley's *Journal* and knew he had encountered numbers of unusual spiritual experiences.

"It's right here," he said, raising the book to a position where we could both see it and tracing with his forefinger as he read. "See, 'John Wesley himself experienced the baptism in the Holy Spirit.' "

"That doesn't state that Wesley spoke in tongues."

"But that's what it means. When you're baptized in the Holy Spirit you *do* speak in tongues. Otherwise, how would you know you had received the Spirit?"

Once more, with patience, I took Mark through the gifts ministries passages in Romans 12, Ephesians 4, and First Corinthians 12 as they related to Acts 2. Once more Mark showed me what he had been taught was incontrovertible evidence, according to Acts 2 and 19 and First Corinthians 14, that apart from tongues there was no valid Holy Spirit baptism. He left in sadness and never tried again.

Toward a Theology of Healing

It was April 1975, when these experiences, along with many others, were brought into clarity of focus by the testimony of Gene Harbison. Before I tried to move the church into a practical ministry of healing, I needed better theological clarification. It was easy enough to document the healing episodes of Jesus from the Gospels. There I saw that the crucial human element in the healing process was faith in God. Now I needed to understand how to transfer New Testament faith concepts into the twentieth

century, when Jesus is no longer physically present.
To reiterate: while Jesus was on earth multitudes of
suffering people received the saving, healing love of
God through Jesus' compassionate touch. That
same healing power has been made available to us
through his reconciling, life-giving death on the
cross. God's redeeming love (1 John 4:10; Rom. 5:8)
has been poured out through the broken body and
shed blood of Christ not only to "save souls" but
also to make the whole person well. According to
First Peter 2:24, "He himself bore our sins in his
body on the tree, so that we might die to sins and
live for righteousness; by his wounds you have been
healed."

In order to understand the way in which the death
of Jesus Christ "on the tree" renders humankind
dead to sin and alive to righteousness, our brokenness healed by the wounds of Christ, we need to
know the cause for this dilemma. As Trevor Dearing
puts it in his book *Supernatural Healing Today:*

> From a Christian point of view, the ultimate cause
> of suffering is man's Fall—his rejection of God. Be-
> cause of this, our love, which was meant to flow to
> God, has turned back upon ourselves. We have been
> self-centered instead of God-centered. Losing the
> unity given by our love for our heavenly Father, full
> of self-love, we have also turned against each other,
> making the world a continual economic, so-
> ciological, military, political and psychological bat-
> tlefield. The Fall has resulted in a disease called sin
> which has affected the whole of humanity. . . . This
> is why our environment seems so hostile and so
> many disasters occur. Men are still as spiritually

desperate as ever. People are bruised and heartbroken by the actions of other sinners, or because of the pressures of a fallen world.

The God of creation had produced a perfect world where unhindered fellowship between God and humanity, between humanity and nature, and among human beings provided perpetually harmonious conditions. When humanity broke fellowship in rebellion against the Creator, every aspect of life was distorted.

The loss of community with God set the world on a spiral of deterioration that could not be reversed apart from a mighty, long-term intervention by the Creator-Redeemer. The heart of that intervention is the atoning work of Jesus Christ, by which the "law of sin and death" is counteracted by the "law of the Spirit of life" (Rom. 8:2).

The more I saw that Christ came to die for our sins so that our loving relationship with God might be restored, the more I realized that healing, in all its aspects, was a by-product of this restoration. I came to think of healing always in the context of a longer phrase: salvation, healing, and wholeness.

Leslie Weatherhead had years earlier defined it in *Psychology, Religion, and Healing* in these terms:

By healing, then, is meant the process of restoring the broken harmony which prevents personality, at any point of body, mind, or spirit, from its perfect functioning in its relevant environment; the body in the material world; the mind in the realm of true ideas and the spirit in its relationship to God.

This definition allows for the process to be supernaturally accelerated to the point of instantaneous healing. It also provides for the flow of God's healing love to move at a slower pace, which gradually results in healing.

Teaching Concepts of Faith for Healing

It has always seemed to me inconsistent for someone to say, "I believe in prayer," and then add, "But I don't believe in healing." I was able to live on both sides of that street for years.

At Wesley Church most of the members believed in prayer. Most of them believed in forgiveness of sins. Not many of them believed in healing. But we prayed for sick people, not sinners.

Here is a typical small-group scene. We're concluding a church meeting, maybe a Bible study. "Any prayer requests?" Several names are mentioned. Problems, mostly having to do with physical ailments, are described. We pray for those persons mentioned, though we don't believe in healing. No one names sinners for whom we should pray. We believe in forgiveness of sins.

The quality and direction of our faith is unquestionably the key to an effective ministry of healing. Misunderstanding about what to believe and how to express faith hinders, even destroys, such a ministry. I began to teach, preach, and talk about a formula and a phrase. The formula: "Perfect love plus perfect faith produce perfect wholeness." (Here we use *perfect* in the sense of complete, or total.) I emphasized that perfect love and perfect wholeness are not our accomplishments. They belong to God. Perfect faith is the part we play in the equation, always aware that as yet our faith is imperfect, incomplete.

The phrase "salvation, healing, and wholeness" has been explained earlier in this book. As I taught faith at Wesley Church, I frequently reminded the people that "whenever you say *healing,* I want you to think of it in terms of 'salvation, healing, and wholeness.' " We developed a few principles about faith for healing.

Faith does not heal. I know that Jesus said on several occasions, "Go thy way. Thy faith has made thee whole" (e.g., Matt. 9:22, KJV). It's like walking into a dark room and flipping the light switch. Light floods the room. You might say your action produced the light. What you did was necessary, but it played a minimal part in the cause-and-effect chain leading to the lighting of the room. Someone else generated the power. The switch at the power plant had already been thrown.

The power for healing is in the Spirit of God. Jesus Christ has already poured his love and life into a dying world by means of the Holy Spirit. Flipping the switch is exercising faith to receive that power. A more accurate analogy might be that of allowing yourself to be the wiring into and through which the energy is received.

But faith is essential. I emphasize distinction between the need for faith and the fact that it does not heal only to keep perspective. It's easy to slip into the fallacy of thinking faith is the healing agent. Then we try hard to have faith. We psych ourselves up to "believe for" our healing. The harder we try, the more closed we are to the flow of the Holy Spirit.

Increased faith is not trying harder but trusting more. All the faith you need, Jesus said, is that of a grain of mustard seed. The key is to focus your faith in God, not in your capacity to believe or in healing or in a healer representing God or in some method of healing.

Let me reiterate and enlarge on the formula mentioned above. "Perfect love plus perfect faith produce perfect wholeness." That thought is an alternate statement of Ephesians 2:8-9, which I quote here with some amplification. "For it is by grace [expressed in God's redeeming, "perfect" love] you have been saved [healed and restored to "perfect" wholeness], through faith [the cooperative part God gives us to play, never perfectly expressed]—and this not from yourselves, it is the gift of God—not by works, so that no one can boast."

Heavy emphasis is given throughout the New Testament that love was God's motivation for sending the Son of God into this sinsick world to be crucified for humanity's redemption (John 3:16; Rom. 5:8; 1 John 4:10). Faith is essentially a trust relationship with a loving heavenly Father. Faith for healing does not convince God to act. God has already acted supremely in Jesus. "He who did not spare his own Son, but gave him up for us all—how will he not also, along with him, graciously give us all things?" (Rom. 8:32). Nothing greater can be done. That is perfect love.

The wholeness God plans for us is conformity to the image of Jesus. "We . . . are being transformed into his likeness with ever-increasing glory, which comes from the Lord, who is the Spirit" (2 Cor. 3:18). "The Lord Jesus Christ, who, by the power that enables him to bring everything under his control, will transform our lowly bodies so that they will be like his glorious body" (Phil. 3:20-21). Conformity to the image of God's Son is perfect wholeness.

When we see wholeness of body, mind, and spirit as God's goal for humankind, we are freed from the narrow definition of healing that forces us to conclude God isn't healing us if we aren't relieved of a given symptom in a prescribed time frame. God is working on more than blind eyes, more than depressed emotions. God is making us completely whole.

If we were altogether free from sin and fear so that total trust in God opened us completely to the power of divine healing love, we would be instantaneously, totally healed. Progress toward perfect faith is our goal.

We can express faith on behalf of those who have none. While I was still a student pastor, an incident in a hospital room gave me insight into this fact. I was visiting a parishioner who suffered from shingles. "Let's have prayer together," I suggested.

"You can if you want to," he answered, "but I don't think it will do any good."

"That's all right. We'll go on my faith this time. There may be a day when my faith is weak, and I'll have to depend on yours." I took his hand in silence for a time. Then I offered a brief thanksgiving for Jesus' love, his understanding of suffering, and his presence with us.

"Oh, thank you," he said. I'm convinced I was not the only one who felt the presence of the Holy Spirit in the room with us.

I was an infant in the faith at that time. I have since

learned something—perhaps only a fragment of the truth—about the extent to which the prayers of other believers have produced healing in my own life. Jesus taught that agreement in prayer of two or three believers produced results. James tells us the fervent prayer of a righteous man is powerful. My experience is that the larger the group—all in the unity of the Spirit—the greater the effects of prayer.

This is not to minimize the value of the sick person's belief. It's great if he or she has it. However, a time of suffering may be just the time when faith is weakest. That doesn't make healing impossible. It only means the channel of faith must be exercised by another believer.

The woman who touched the hem of Jesus' garment received healing through her own faith (Matt. 9:20-22). The centurion's servant received healing through the centurion's faith (Luke 7:1-10). The lame man at the Beautiful Gate was healed through the faith of Peter (Acts 3:1-10). The paralytic brought to Jesus by his friends was healed through *their* faith (Luke 5:17-26). A study of the healing episodes in the Gospels shows that many were healed with no indication of faith on their own part.

Often an ill person is more anxious and fearful than prayerful. He must learn to depend on others for the faith that opens receiving channels for God's abiding presence and healing love.

There are many ways to express faith for healing. The Bible is a book that tells the history of people learning to trust God. They learned by trial and error, success and failure, obedience and apostasy. When you read it intent on discovering the ways they expressed faith, you will be amazed at their variety.

Active faith is a trust relationship with God expressed in an intentional way. The more you use it, the more it grows strong and healthy. When the Hebrew children of God trusted themselves to divine leadership and followed God in obedience, their confidence in God grew. Whenever we do what we believe to be God's will, we are acting in faith. Obedience is a primary expression of faith.

We see God's people expressing faith by praise and worship, sacrifice and thanksgiving. Reading the word of God and hearing it preached are expressions of faith. Congregations evidence faith as they work together for peace and justice, feed the hungry, clothe the poor, visit those in prison.

The most direct expression of faith demonstrated and taught in the scriptures is prayer. Here we enter intimate communion with the Creator.

There are several other expressions of faith that relate directly to the ministry of healing. They are laying on of hands, anointing, and confession of sin.

A study of New Testament healings will show that no one method was used. Sometimes Jesus reached out and touched the person, as he did the leper (Luke 5:13). Sometimes he gave an instruction, "Stretch out your hand" (Matt. 12:13). Once he applied spittle to a man's eyes (Mark 8:23). Sometimes Peter gave a command: "In the name of Jesus of Nazareth, walk" (Act 3:6). People on whom Peter's shadow fell were healed (Acts 5:15).

This partial list of healing methods is provided to disabuse us of the idea that there is one exclusive way or pattern that is right for healing and that other ways are wrong. The issue is to express intentional faith. That is what provides the channel through which the healing love of God is free to flow.

The problems that faith healing addresses are essentially spiritual. Human sin is the basic cause of all maladies. I can get angry when that truth is invested in a pile of stones and cast in lack of discernment at a suffering child of God. Nevertheless, sin and suffering are not God's will for human beings. Glorious, intimate, holy relationships with God and with one another are God's desire for us.

"The wages of sin is death" (Rom. 6:23). That is immediate death to life-giving fellowship with the Spirit of Jesus in any given segment of life. It is also irreversible slow dying to the rest of the body, mind, and spirit. For this reason forgiveness of individual sin, received by faith, is the basic need for all of us when we suffer brokenness of any kind. Healing here is restoration of faith intimacy with God. It is a matter of the spirit.

But there is another kind of sin for which the individual is not directly responsible. It is the "visiting the iniquity of the fathers upon the children to the third and fourth generation of those that hate me" (Exod. 20:5). The antidote to the death of this kind of sin is often called healing of the memories. It relates to the psyche, the soul, the mind. It has to do with the unhealthy psychological mechanisms programmed into all of us by living in families that put their trust in idols. Idols are anything which supersede in our trust priority the Creator-Redeemer God revealed through Jesus Christ.

I was once employed as an Aid to Families with Dependent Children caseworker for the Department of Public Aid in Illinois. It was not uncommon for a client to be the third or fourth generation in a succession of unwed mothers. A familial, as well as sociological, pattern had developed.

Consider this scenario. Dad and Mom, despite their regular involvement in church, are concerned more about financial security than anything else. They drive toward it year after year. It is their idol. How does that affect the basic values programmed into their children? Or what if the parents have no other goal but to satisfy their desire for pleasure? Or they live in a constant state of anxiety? Hostility? Lust? You can extend the list. The point is that something happens in the children to warp their personalities and subject them to potential psychological trauma of many kinds, some of which will result in emotional illness.

Again the cause is sin, but not the sin of the progeny. In these cases inner healing is called for. Usually the psychological warping produces sinful behavior. For example, persons with low self-esteem, the result of parenting that had no time for hands-on love, may become severely depressed. The depression results in irresponsibility. They're told about their sin. They already feel guilty. They confess their sin and try harder, only to discover that the hurts are deeper. The depression persists. They feel guilty. They confess. They try harder. They fail, *ad infinitum*. Do these persons need forgiveness of sin or healing of depression?

They need both. But if the confession of sin is a desperate expression of agony over a lifetime of perceived failure, it is more a pitiful self-effort to throw off the feeling of condemnation than it is heartfelt repentance over conviction of sin. It is more likely to be an expression of despair rather than faith in the love and forgiveness of Jesus.

He or she needs a series, perhaps gradual, of alternate healing and forgiveness. Each modicum of healing brings strength to see the truth about that area of life. It is the truth of God, ministered by the convicting power of the Holy Spirit, that leads to godly repentance, forgiveness, and God's life in that area so it can be fresh, clean, and strong. At the outset this person must be the recipient of loving faith expressed by others, so the alternate healings and forgiveness can begin to reverse a spiritually and emotionally immobilized condition. This is a matter primarily of healing for the mind.

There is yet a third factor in human existence that is potentially malevolent. We live in a fallen, "cursed" creation. Natural law is subject to unpredictable aberrations. This is not the perfectly harmonious Garden of Eden setting in which human beings, created in the image of God, are free to frolic in happy fellowship with God and with one another.

The disobedient choice of our first ancestors to become godlike in their perception of the knowledge of good and evil led to a curse of thorns, barren earth, and difficult childbirth (Gen. 3:1-19). Just as the Genesis account of created animals is only suggestive of all God made, so these evils are only suggestive of all the natural maladies now extant in what once was a wholly "good" creation. There are natural imperfections of many kinds, such as infectious disease, disasters of earthquake and wind, and the diabolical influence of the powers of darkness (Eph. 6:12). These malignant forces pro-

vide plenty of ammunition for attacking the physical lives of human beings even if their emotional
and spiritual lives were functioning in perfect harmony.

Jesus gave his disciples a lesson on faith. "Have
faith in God," he said. He talked about being able to
cast a mountain into the sea if you believe. Then he
told them, "Therefore I tell you, whatever you ask
for in prayer, believe that you have received it, and it
will be yours" (Mark 11:24). I've heard preachers
develop this promise in ways that castigate those
who do not *have* what they prayed for, whether it be
prosperity or healing. Either they don't trust the
words of Jesus or they don't really believe.

I suggest that Jesus expected his hearers to be
aware of the three conditions listed above, sins of
the spirit, damaged emotions, and "cursed" nature,
when they formulate what they can realistically believe. That doesn't mean that God has left us helpless. Quite the contrary. God sent Jesus, the only
Son, to minister to us at the heart of these very
needs. It is in this context that we activate faith for
healing.

We can't pray God into healing any more than we
can talk the sun into shining. Just as light and heat
are streaming earthward from the sun, so God's
healing love has been poured out through the death
of Jesus Christ on the cross. However, we don't
always see the sun. It may be hidden behind clouds.
So God's healing love may not be received because
clouds of sin and doubt stand between. Faith pokes
holes in those clouds not to get the love to flow but
to make openings through which it can enter into

this dark world of sin and suffering. The healing
love is always available by God's grace. We receive it
by opening a channel of faith.

Avoiding Polarization of Church Members

I was eager to introduce an intentional ministry of
healing at Wesley Church. But I was just as concerned to avoid polarization over this issue. Two
problems appeared. The first, and broader, possibility was that there could be divided loyalties over the
decision of whether or not to offer healing services.
A second was the potential problem, already at a
minor hum, between traditionalists and charismatics. I didn't want the healing ministry to be seen as a
conflict between opposing factions.

A plan gradually evolved for low-key education
and an "exploration," or pilot experience, in holding
one service of healing. It was only natural for me to
tell the story of Gene Harbison whenever an opportunity arose. That was a right step. My weekly newsletter editorials occasionally referred to the ministry
of healing or the charismatic movement. Sermon
illustrations that told of God's healing love were
highlighted rather than used in passing to make
some other point.

I had learned that a surgeon friend of Gene Harbison's from Peoria, Dr. William Griffin, himself a
Cursiesta, once led a seminar with Gene to provide
a medical perspective on the ministry of healing. It
seemed to me that these two men might play an
important role in introducing that ministry at
Wesley.

A phone call to Gene confirmed that they had

done that, along with a third witness, Hobe Albright, and would be glad to come to our church when we needed them. I began to think in terms of an autumn launching date for this experiment.

In planning my autumn preaching schedule, I penciled in two sermons about the formula and the phrase explained above. These we used in preparation for the Sunday of testimonies by Harbison, Albright, and Griffin. It seemed to me that these visitors should be introduced not as God's directive word for our situation but as part of a larger exploration into where the Lord may be leading Wesley Church. *Exploration* was the word I needed. We would call that Sunday an "Exploration in Spiritual Healing."

As the plan developed, there were to be two gatherings in addition to morning worship. In the afternoon we would have a panel discussion on the merits of providing an intentional ministry of healing for Wesley Church. That evening we would hold an experimental healing service.

For weeks prior to the chosen Sunday we announced from the pulpit, talked during the week, and wrote in the newsletter about the "Exploration in Spiritual Healing." There was plenty of opportunity in advance for everyone who was interested to think, talk, and pray about the possibility of initiating an intentional ministry of healing.

On "Exploration" day Hobe Albright served as the emcee. His introductory comments set the direction for each of the other talks. The presentation was dignified, informative, and, from my point of view, electrifying. It was a powerful presentation of the gospel of Jesus Christ.

Fifty people showed up for the panel discussion. In addition to the three guests and myself, I had invited two respected members of the congregation to join us on the panel. It was all very calm, with little interaction from the congregation during the question-and-answer time.

The highlight of the day was the healing service. Nearly a hundred worshipers, many of them from other churches, arrived in an expectant, prayerful mood. I offered a brief homily on the healing love of God, we celebrated the Holy Communion, and then I invited those who desired prayer to return to the communion rail and kneel. This went on for an hour as I moved back and forth laying on hands and praying for people.

Two days later a lady phoned to tell me she had been to her physician on Monday and learned that her diabetes was healed. For weeks I received positive feedback from persons who had been greatly blessed by the service, several of whom described specific healings. How we praised God!

Choosing the Worship Style for Our Healing Services

My exposure to the ministry of healing had given me three possible models to choose from and adapt for Wesley Church. 1) There was that first healing service I had attended in the Episcopal church. The Eucharist had been observed. The priests did the praying. 2) There were healing rallies like the one where I had fallen "under the power." Spirit-filled leaders, gifted for healing, led the praise service and prayed for the sick. 3) I had also been in churches (like the Church of the Redeemer in Houston) where praying for the sick occurred on almost any occasion. Laypersons and/or the pastors prayed for those in need of being healed. I thought of these as 1) the Sacramental model, 2) the Praise Rally model, and 3) the Body Life model.

The definition of "salvation, healing, and wholeness" that we had been teaching tended to bias me in favor of the Sacramental model. A service that centers in the atoning work of Jesus Christ on the cross rather than in the gifts ministry of the Holy Spirit seems to me more faithful to the New Testament message. Of course, it can't be either/or. This is a both/and matter. The question is one of selecting the focus of faith.

The Praise Rally puts emphasis on the operation of the gifts of the Spirit through anointed leaders. These services are powerfully effective. The encouragement to expect miracles raises the level of genuine faith, and many are healed. However, the only kind of healing that can be observed is physical. Spiritual and emotional healings, even when they occur instantaneously, as they often do, must be proven over time. There tends to be more emphasis on the external and dramatic dimensions of healing. Along with this emphasis there can be a subtle shift of perspective that gives more attention to the gifted healer and flamboyant activity than to the heart of the matter, what Jesus Christ has done for humankind on the cross.

For this reason I preferred the kind of service developed over the years by such groups as the International Order of St. Luke the Physician. Worship is centered in the Eucharist. Jesus Christ is pre-eminent. His brokenness is dramatized. His shed blood is consecrated according to his command. The Lamb of God who takes away the sins of the world is honored. The participants take time to confess, repent, and be washed clean of all sin. They are prepared spiritually, emotionally, and physically to receive the healing love of God.

Several months after the "Exploration in Spiritual Healing," we began holding Communion and Healing services in the chapel the first Sunday evening of each month. The service included a brief period of hymn singing, a short homily on one of the healing episodes of Jesus, an informal liturgy of Holy Communion, and prayers for healing.

My associate pastor and I presided, each at a short kneeling bench. Participants would come forward, state their need, and kneel. We anointed them, placed our hands on their head, and prayed extemporaneously as the Spirit led. Usually about thirty people attended. Always there was a rich sense of the presence of God. We were blessed by God's Spirit.

I had heard of a few heated discussions that had occurred during our nine months of preparation for launching an intentional ministry of healing at Wesley Church. However, there was no widespread disagreement apparent in the church. Those who remained skeptical were gracious in honoring the participants. Those who appreciated the services never demeaned the others. By God's grace the intentional ministry of healing had been established. It was becoming the heart of a healthy body.

SO FAR . . .

- We embrace a definition of healing that is broad enough to include the whole person—body, mind, and spirit—and which allows for gradual as well as instantaneous results.
- We endorse a theology of healing which places greater faith emphasis in the atoning work of Christ than in the gift ministries of the Holy Spirit. This is not to minimize the latter but to provide instruction for deciding what form the healing services should take.
- We provide education and information about the ministry of healing in a low-key way over a period of months, including an opportunity to explore what a service of healing would be like. This gave opportunity for input and feedback from members of the congregation after they had had time to think, talk it over, and pray about it in non-threatening situations of their own choosing.
- We are careful to avoid having our consideration about the possibility of launching an intentional ministry of healing become a charismatic/traditionalist issue.
- The Sacrament of Holy Communion provides a sacred, effective means for persons to experience assurance of forgiveness, inner peace, and faith-generated openness to receive God's healing love.
- The anointing, laying on of hands, and prayers for healing by ordained elders assume a sacramental tone as they are carried out in obedience to scriptural direction.
- The intentional ministry of healing has been established as an integral and important part of the

church's program without polarizing the congregation.

For Reflection and Discussion

1. The author believes the phrase *charismatic Christian* is redundant. Do you agree? How would those in your circle of friends define *Christian*? How do some people differentiate charismatic Christians from other Christians?

2. The author urged members of his congregation to think of healing in the larger context of "salvation, healing, and wholeness of body, mind, and spirit." Does this bury healing so much that it loses meaning? What value do you see in describing healing as one part of a larger process? What is your definition of healing?

3. What would you say to a faith-healing practitioner who told a diseased person that the reason he/she was not healed was lack of faith? Do you agree that persons who are not personally expressing faith for healing can be healed through the faith of other believers?

4. The author is eager to differentiate between focusing faith in healing and focusing faith in God, the Healer. How can one tell the difference between believing in healing and trusting God for healing? Do you agree this distinction is important?

5. Suppose your church were to consider the possibility of starting an intentional ministry of healing. What gradual steps of education would be helpful to avoid polarization of those with different opinions?

CHAPTER 5

The Ministry of the Laity

Starting Over

In June of 1979 my bishop said move, so I
moved, moved to a downtown church in a city of
ninety thousand inhabitants. The church had polar-
ized and split over the charismatic issue. Contrary
to many church splits, in which the charismatics
form their own group and begin a new church, the
traditionalists were the group to leave. One hundred and twenty (they relished the numbers identity with those waiting in the upper room for the Holy
Spirit to birth the New Testament church in
Jerusalem) old-guard members left Central United
Methodist Church under the leadership of the associate pastor. They called themselves Emmanuel
(emphasizing "God with *us*") Methodist Church,
Interdenominational. I was now the directing pastor
at Central.

At first, I thought that introducing the intentional

ministry of healing at Central would be simple and well received. That priority soon faded into the background while I dealt with more immediate felt needs. Men and women, strong in the faith, were bewildered and hurt over the split. The wounds from painful accusations and recriminations were evident. Mutual trust level was low. The need was for gradual rebuilding of trust and purpose. I decided to work toward establishing small groups for discipleship and koinonia.

Whenever I move, I start over, in a lot of ways. One of them is to throw out all the lettered signs and mottos that I've scotchtaped and tacked to the desk and walls of my den and begin a fresh series. In our new house the first sign I put up was a quote from Oswald Chambers in his book *My Utmost for His Highest,* "The measure of the worth of our public activity for God is the private profound communion we have with Him."

Shortly thereafter I summed up much of my learning experience as a pastor into an understanding of my task at Central. "The measure of the worth of my effectiveness as pastor at Central will be the extent to which we bring our saints into spiritual growth and active ministry, including leadership."

Years earlier the motive for that goal had come into focus for me while reading about a baseball team. The manager had been impressed by a young catcher with a strong batting average in spring training. The manager announced that the young player would replace the veteran catcher that year.

The team lost their opening game. Twice the young catcher grounded out feebly with men on base. Once he wandered around under a pop foul which dropped between his outstretched hands. The next day the veteran catcher played.

The third day was a rainout. The sports writers grilled the manager about his failure to give the young catcher a fair chance. "He'll be back," the manager said. "You guys'll never guess why I didn't play him yesterday. In fact, I'll give you ten tries. Here's a five-dollar bill for the one who comes up with the answer."

He wrote something on a piece of paper and turned it over on his desk. Writer after writer called out one or another of the young catcher's deficiencies. After ten wrong guesses the wise old manager turned up the note. "Not enjoying himself," he said. "I don't want anyone in the lineup who isn't enjoying the game."

A light of recognition went on for me. It was perplexing to see men and women whose faith in Jesus Christ was of far greater depth and duration than my own who weren't enjoying the game. It was great fun for me. I wanted them to enjoy it, too.

Instead, their church work often seemed to be drudgery for them. At best they had withdrawn and settled into a life of indifference to the exciting adventure of accomplishing God's mission moment by moment in a challenging world.

I often pondered this fact. Gradually it occurred to me that my joy came from being in cooperative ministry with the Lord Jesus. They didn't *know* that they were in ministry, too. They thought their job was to pay and pray and sit in the pews so *I* could do the ministering!

No wonder people got bored and became spiritual and/or physical dropouts! Imagine discovering the reality of the living God at work in your life! You want to serve God with this new-found vitality. You're ready to make a difference in this chaotic world, to minister the love and life of Jesus to those around you.

You're a banker, so they put you on the finance committee and leave you there until you retire. You're a sales representative, so they make you an usher. You're a great homemaker, so you work in the church kitchen at the annual bazaar.

You read about the "people ministry" of Jesus and his disciples, about the Holy Spirit excitement of the Book of Acts. Nothing like that is happening in the lives of the Christians in your church, except, perhaps, in the life of the pastor.

You're willing to leave everything to become a missionary or a pastor, but you don't have a "call." You give up and drudge it out on the finance committee, as an usher, or on the kitchen patrol. Church is a bore. There is too little vitality for a healthy body.

Of course, those activities, as well as scores of other necessary tasks in the church, can be Holy-Spirit ministries. Usually they're not experienced that way. They've been handled without the Spirit's power for so long that no one has thought to call on the Spirit for guiding the finance committee, for pouring out the Spirit's vitality through the ushers, for making Jesus excitingly real in the church bazaar.

For sure, no one has prepared you to go in the powerful name of Jesus to witness to a street gang or pray for healing in the homes of sick members or tell a despairing friend at work how to receive Christ.

We have failed to teach our church members how to be Spirit-filled channels through whom the healing love of God can flow in powerful ways.

My primary role at Wesley Church had become that of the equipping pastor (Eph. 4:11-16). We began to help Christians mature in the faith so they could discover their spiritual gifts and let the Holy Spirit empower them for effective ministry. As they came to life in the Spirit we were able to assimilate them into body-life at the church, husband that life toward conformity to the image of God's Son, equip them for a variety of gifted ministries, and turn them loose in the name of the Lord Jesus.

The Charismatic Impact

The revolution of a bored laity hit Central Church in a different way and with much greater impact. It was situated at the center of a hotbed of charismatic renewal rather than at the periphery. Its city was one of the first to benefit from a cable TV channel that broadcast Christian programming with a Pentecostal bias twenty-four hours a day. It had been led by a dynamic pastor whose forte was evangelistic preaching. Freshly "baptized in the Holy Spirit," Christians from all denominations, frustrated by dead churches, packed their way into this little church to taste of the power of God's moving Spirit.

The more the worship services were punctuated with demonstrations of spiritual power in terms of charismatic praise, testimony, healing, falling under the power, and exorcisms, the stronger rose the resistance in the hearts of those whose forebears had established and nurtured the church. They couldn't handle the rapid change any longer. Many of them departed. The gifted pastor was called into full-time evangelistic work.

I was appointed to bring unity to this diverse assemblage, now comprised mostly of an influx of new charismatics, a recalcitrant group of old-guard members who refused to be driven out, and another group of perplexed, concerned people seeking to bring peace and order.

Under my leadership miracles ceased. Within days the thrill-seekers looked elsewhere for more exciting praise rallies. Within weeks charismatics began drifting away. Income was halved. We revised the budget downward by 50 percent. People from both camps lined up at my study door with advice to stem the tide.

One outspoken charismatic who had come to Central from a "dead" United Methodist church summed it up for me. "All the Spirit-filled people are leaving," he announced, "because they're not getting fed."

Since he was the third one to supply this crucial information in a week and because my frustration level was extremely high, my response was undoubtedly caustic. I was under the impression that by this time most of the fly-by-nighters were gone. I knew my biblical preaching had been considered bread in previous pastorates. "Give me a list of the people," I said. "And tell me what you mean by 'getting fed.' "

"Well, I can't exactly tell you who all they are. But we're not seeing miracles any more. Miracles are what build faith, and they're just not happening the way we worship these days." This information was one of the most important clues I received about our problems. I had always thought that "faith cometh by hearing, and hearing by the Word of God" (Rom. 10:17, KJV), which I was preaching.

This was an educational turning point for me. With great relief I relinquished a large part of my sense of failure. This was not my fault. With some sense of triumph, I'm sure, I happily responded, "I can't produce miracles. That's God's business." He and his family went to another church.

Important as it was for me to grasp this aspect of my inability to meet the charismatic expectations, there was another learning experience even more instructive. I began to overhear statements like, "We all know our needs are no longer being met here. We'll just have to start meeting one another's needs."

I knew what they meant by meeting needs. That was companion to the experience of miracles. Miracles occurred and needs were met when, through preaching, praise, word of knowledge, message in tongues, or some other supernatural intervention from on high, one or many among the members of the congregation were convicted of need, went to the altar, and *through the ministry of a Spirit-filled worker,* were touched by God, "needs" met.

For some months prior to my administration, worship services had been geared for the meeting of needs in this way. The pastor had discontinued use of an order of worship in the belief that such structure inhibited the freedom of the Holy Spirit to move in meeting needs. The ideal service was one in which, from beginning to end, people were going to and from the altar, being healed, falling under the power, and finding their needs met by the manifest power of the Holy Spirit. I yearned for those results, but had no idea what to do about it.

A number of people were conscientious in trying to educate me. They resisted my use of an order of worship. They showed me where to stand and what to say so that worshipers would be motivated to go to the altar. To no avail. I seemed unwilling, or unable, to learn.

But I was learning. I was learning that the charismatic influence at Central—and I extrapolated this application to the movement in general—was rightfully saying to the clergy and church, "We want a piece of the action. We're not going to sit back any longer and let the professionals have all the fun. The Lord God intends for *all* of us to be in ministry, not just those with full-time salaried positions."

They were saying what I knew. What the New Testament taught, what the church needed, and what the Lord was doing in these exciting days was to empower the laity. Now we needed to find the Lord's way to get it together.

The Gift of Discerning of Spirits

Two things in the experience of worship at Central in those days were especially bothersome to me. Some of the good people who thought miracles were the primary evidence of meaningful worship seemed to be helping God out. I was suspicious that they were manifesting such supernatural gifts as tongues, interpretation, prophecy, and falling under the power with a little help from the flesh.

In the second place, the theology of worship which I espoused put a lot more emphasis on celebrating the mighty historic acts of God, especially the resurrection of Jesus Christ from the dead on the first day of the week, than on getting our needs met. I was hungry to see needs met, but I believed that we were most likely open to allow the power of God to touch our lives when we reversed the focus.

To put it another way, those worshipers who were constantly checking their spiritual pulse and seeking goose-bump experiences tended to become subjective, involuted. We were called each Lord's Day to remember the life, death, and resurrection of Jesus Christ in terms of awe, mystery, and wonder. Granted, that same awe is engendered by a contemporary miracle, but the resurrection of Jesus was validated over a period of time. I was looking for greater validation that these miracles were supernatural rather than psychologically induced. There was an unhealthy quality about the vitality of this Body.

The gift most necessary for our condition was that of discerning of spirits. Ten years earlier I had come across two books about supernatural events in the community of faith gathered around the Church of the Redeemer, an Episcopalian church in Houston.

The old guard at Redeemer adamantly sought to preserve their identity as a liturgically high church. But the neighborhood was rapidly changing from a wealthy residential area near downtown to a run-down section populated by Mexican Americans. The Episcopalians who continued to worship there drove in from the suburbs.

When Graham Pulkingham, a young rector from

Austin, succeeded the man who retired, he wanted
to minister to the neighborhood. This precipitated a
mass exodus of the former members and left the
church empty.

To greatly abbreviate the story, Pulkingham received the baptism in the Holy Spirit, miracles began happening around him, and crowds of thrill-
seekers came in. As the difficult ministry of meeting
desperate human need in the community became
apparent, the chaff drifted away, too. What remained was a group of people "gathered for power,"
as the book title puts it.

Lives were being redeemed and healed. They
sought to address the needs of their blighted neighborhood by purchasing homes, moving into them
as "households," renovating the homes as they
worked together, and seeing lives literally remade
by the power of the Holy Spirit.

Members began a ministry to the school across
the street, tutoring the slow, helping those with
problems, working as volunteer playground super-
visors and room mothers. They established a medical and dental clinic which served scores of poor
people every day. They fed and clothed hundreds of
needy people, not to mention miraculous healings
of body, mind, and spirit. It was like reading a
twentieth-century Book of Acts.

I made two trips to Houston in the mid-seventies
to observe the community effect of Christian living
there. By this time eighty homes near the church
had been purchased by church members and populated with a mixture of mature Christians and struggling beginners, most of whom had severe problems of one kind or another. For example, it was

common for local courts to send teenagers with criminal records to live in this Christian environment. One-parent families made up much of the household population.

Each household was presided over by a head couple, who gave direction, counsel, and stability to the family of Christians in that particular house. It was an intense setting in which to apply the principles of New Testament living.

Paul Patton, who had been a veterinarian in Oklahoma prior to his call to the Redeemer Community, was the head of the household where I stayed for a few days. His assignment in the community was to oversee all the plumbing repairs. More importantly, he was one of the elders of the community. That group met each morning to seek the direction of the Lord for the church and its ministry.

Paul took me aside for an informal interview my first evening at Patton House. Later I realized this was for the purpose of discovering any spiritual needs they might be empowered to meet in my life while I was with them. Hundreds of people were involved in the community. Some worked away from the church and pooled their salaries for the household expenses. Many worked in and around the community in ministries assigned them on the basis of their gifts.

There was constant spiritual ferment and challenge to the ministry at Redeemer. As Paul asked me about my gifts, he made the comment that there was one gift more in demand than any other. It was the gift of "discerning of spirits" (1 Cor. 12:10). The community needed to be sure in that dynamic culture whether or not what they were seeing and experiencing in any given situation was diabolical, of the flesh, or of the Holy Spirit.

Trying to Find Our Balance

At Central I sought the same gift. There were a few saints who seemed to need to call attention to themselves regularly by manifesting gifts. I felt they were demonstrating their own immaturity more than they were edifying the Body. I wanted neither to quench the Holy Spirit nor to wound their human spirit by publicly declaring them out of order.

Alice was one who had a message for the Body every Sunday (and every other time there was a meeting). I began to meet with her during each week for prayer and conversation. She reluctantly agreed to check with me prior to Sunday worship so that I might validate in advance her "word from the Lord."

About a year after my arrival at Central Church I was out of town one Sunday. Alice came to the lectern following the associate pastor's sermon and addressed the congregation. I heard about it but did not see her to discuss the problem with her.

Two Sundays later, as Don was approaching the lectern for the scripture reading, Alice stood and offered a lengthy message in tongues. Don waited for her to finish and then read the word. I was praying for discernment but had no confirmation one way or the other. The congregation seemed restless and confused. I stepped into the pulpit to preach. To my surprise, yet with total composure, I stated matter of factly, "I want the congregation to know that tongue was out of order."

With that I prayed and delivered my sermon, which I also concluded with prayer. In the silence following the prayer a friend of Alice's stood. "Pastor," she called out from across the room, "I want you to know that tongue was not out of order. I had the interpretation, but Don didn't give me a chance to give it. May I give it now?"

"No," I said and announced the hymn of invitation. The congregation was subdued following the benediction. There were mixed reactions. Some said, "I don't understand why you did that," as they filed past me. Others said, "I'm glad you did that." Most made no comment at all.

It was a watershed event for our worship services. Alice and her friends left the church. Word gifts were gone for months. We went through a long period of reconstruction as the congregation came into more unified expressions of worship.

I began to teach on the importance of an objective focus for our worship services. The charismatics had learned that *liturgy* was a dirty word, that an order of worship of our own doing forced God out of the service. I tried to tell them that a service was comprised both of structure and of spontaneity, that no service was without a semblance of structure, that without structure, spontaneity had no setting in which to take place. The proper question to ask was not whether we should have a liturgy, since there could be no worship without it. Our task was to find the optimum expression of worship by which this particular Body of Christ could most effectively glorify God. To glorify God, I claimed, was humankind's paramount purpose in life. We must prepare ourselves to enter worship thinking, *What can I put into this?* rather than *I don't get anything out of this.*

I taught that liturgy, whatever the worship style (including praise rallies), was "the work of the people." I urged members of the congregation to think first in terms of what they might have to offer Christ in praise, thanksgiving, adoration, and self that would bring glory to God's name in the assembled congregation.

Television productions, Holy Spirit conventions, praise rallies, and a variety of other charismatic experiences had fed the distorted implication that worship should be evaluated on the basis of demonstrated emotional/spiritual response. Every song, every word, every sermon became an object for thumbs up or thumbs down, the good ones receiving applause.

Kierkegaard shook Copenhagen with the message that their practice of viewing the clergy as performers on a stage, acting on behalf of God for the approval of the audience, was a reversal of the truth. The congregation is on-stage performing for the benefit of God, who is the audience. The clergy are merely prompters in the wings whispering occasional instructions to the actors.

Despite the fact that Central was richly gifted with high quality musicians, preaching, and creative scripture-oriented themes for our services, every worship committee meeting included unhappy discussion about the order of worship being too tight for God to get in. I continued to encourage a theology of worship that emphasized the life, death, and resurrection of the Lord Jesus, so that as we walked through the challenges of each week we would have fresh remembrance of God's resurrection power. My position was that confidence in the resurrection validates the atoning work of Jesus and engenders faith in the God of victories for whatever graveyard experiences we meet during the week.

I also reaffirmed my eager desire to hear from the Lord through word gifts during the services. Their position was that for this to happen I, as worship leader, must encourage gifts ministries; I must prime the pump, so to speak. I believed that would cater to fleshly expressions, that the Lord was just being silent in those charismatic ways with us at this time.

Wesleyan Roots for Charismatics

By this time in my Christian experience I was appreciative of, but not bound by, Wesley's understanding of grace and his emphasis on the doctrines of perfection and assurance. The Doctrinal Studies Commission established just prior to the merger between the Methodist church and the Evangelical United Brethren church emphasized Wesley's quadrilateral parameters for doing theology. They reaffirmed his view that scripture, tradition, reason, and experience were the guidelines within which we were free to theologize.

It pained me that so few Pentecostals acknowledged their Wesleyan roots, deep in the soil of what he called "scriptural holiness," as the source of the modern Pentecostal movement. I found the charismatics generally unwilling to listen to anything they thought was denominational. They were especially unsympathetic to Methodism, considering it an apostate church.

On the other hand, I could not understand why United Methodists so often disdained Pentecostals. Many of my peers considered the charismatics to be immature malcontents, preoccupied with their own spiritual pulse and emotional highs and preferring running around to praise rallies over digging in on the hard tasks of serving the Lord in steadfast ministry. I had learned that while this may be true of a few charismatics, especially those less mature, most were a vital force for God's effective ministry in the church.

Toward a Healthy Body

My priority was to work toward healthy functioning of the Body of Christ in its local expression, to find Spirit-led biblical ways to make it more Christlike. I was eager to see the healing life and love of Jesus—so graciously poured out on humankind by his life, death, and resurrection—flow through his Body by the agency of the Holy Spirit. I was both Wesleyan *and* neo-Pentecostal, with a strong aversion to any position which declared them incompatible.

By compatibility, however, I did not mean a compromise that required everyone to espouse like doctrine. I acknowledged the success quotient of church-growth literature which recommended the homogeneous unit principle: build the church on like-minded people with common goals, and it will grow. I thought the New Testament represented a willingness to battle out differences as long as the essential unity under the headship of Christ was maintained.

J. B. Phillips translated Romans 12:2, "Don't let the world around you squeeze you into its own mold, but let God remold your minds from within." My observation of many churches was that *they*, at least as much as the world, were the control agents trying to squeeze everyone into conformity.

Occasionally, I would diagram this for classes by making line drawings of people of various shapes marching single file into churches of several different denominations. From one church they all filed out in the shape of circles; from another they all emerged star-shaped; those coming out of the third were square. Everyone who stayed around for very long in the same church was into the form that church required of its adherents. They either dropped out or were made uncomfortable until they conformed.

This was a setup for teaching our goal at Central for each individual to maintain his or her unique identity, but to increasingly conform that identity to the image of God's Son (Rom. 8:29), changed into his likeness (2 Cor. 3:18).

The purpose of the church, we taught, was to glorify God. The supreme way to bring glory to God was for the Body to become increasingly Christlike, individually and corporately.

A healthy Body of Christ would be one that functioned in love and truth under the headship of Jesus; that increasingly grew in the same sensitivity to human need that Jesus felt as he strode the streets

of Jerusalem or walked along the shores of Galilee;
that had ears attuned to hear from the Creator, announcing the kingdom of light as the antidote to this
world's kingdom of darkness and calling persons to
repent and believe this good news; that received
sight to see, as Jesus did, whether a traumatized
person first needed healing or confrontation about
sin; that appropriated faith power with which to
confront and cast out evil; that grew up, in short, to
all the fullness of the stature of Christ.

Jesus of Nazareth, of Capernaum, of Jerusalem, of
the Sea of Galilee and the hills above it—and of
Golgotha—was our model. Paul's letter to the
church at Ephesus was our primary handbook. At
this stage in the history of Central the first priority
became Body building.

Body building would have been greatly facilitated
if I could have simply chosen the "right" theology
and laid it on the church in regular sermonic doses.
There is a great advantage to definite positioning.
Everyone knows (or can easily find the official literature by which to learn) exactly what we are to
believe and how we are to behave. Unfortunately, I
had never been able to discover *the* systematic biblical theology. I was familiar with several, friends
with some; but the truth kept coming back to me in
terms of a Person, and I couldn't squeeze God into a
doctrinal position.

It is reported that Rufus Mosely once went to
discuss a doctrinal matter with a seminary professor. Rufus was spending a few days on campus
doing library research. He was dismayed to hear
this professor express doubt in a chapel talk about

the doctrine of the virgin birth, so he made an appointment to talk it over with the professor.

They exchanged views. The professor argued that the word for *virgin* could just as well be translated "young woman." Mosely reasoned that the "fully human, fully God" view of Christ required a divine parent. Neither could be persuaded by the other.

Finally Rufus said, "Why don't we just ask him whether he was born of a virgin or not?"

"How would we do that?" asked the startled professor.

"Just bow your head and pray."

They both bowed in silence for a few minutes. At last Rufus asked, "Well, what did he say?"

"Nothing," the professor answered. "What did he say to you?"

"He allowed as how he was born of a virgin, but said we need to be very patient with those who haven't discovered it yet."

Central needed a sense of identity. Prior to the Methodist-EUB merger of 1968 her identity was *First* Evangelical United Brethren. That name had to be changed, since "First" was retained by the Methodist church which had been "first." Before the split, Central was fond of describing herself as an oasis, meaning a place where persons from various dry churches could come to be refreshed in the life-giving stream of the Holy Spirit.

Learning to Love

We sought a theme that would overarch several theological positions, an umbrella that would be wide enough to canopy a variety of dreams, goals, and purposes. It turned out to be "A Church That Is Learning to Love."

The learning theme was tri-faceted: learning to love the Lord ("Love the Lord your God with all your heart and with all your soul and with all your mind," Matt. 22:37); learning to love one another ("A new command I give you: Love one another. As I have loved you, so you must love one another," John 13:34); and learning to love the world for whom Christ died ("May the Lord make your love increase and overflow for each other and for everyone else," 1 Thess. 3:12).

To use the word *learning* in no way implied we weren't doing that. It simply acknowledged there was continual room for growth in our capacity to love. It also picked up on the definition of a disciple as a learner of Jesus.

The three learning emphases roughly paralleled the three functions of a church: worship, nurture, and outreach. My view was that nurture, defined at Central now as "learning to love one another" (and in my mind as Body building), was the area most needing careful attention. In addition to the usual nurturing functions of a church, we addressed this task through fostering discipleship and koinonia groups.

Of course, we didn't view this love-one-another process as an end in itself. We were convinced that both worship and outreach would be enhanced by individuals in the body becoming stronger through bearing one another's burdens and holding one another accountable for maturing in Christlikeness.

The Need for Discipling

It had been at least fifteen years since I first realized the need to equip the laity for ministry. I knew that laypersons in my denomination were unlikely to be biblically trained. My early attempts at discipling centered in small prayer and Bible study groups. If it worked for Jesus and the disciples, for Wesley and the classes, it should work for us.

Groups varied in size, makeup, motivation, and duration. I received little positive feedback from most of these groups. Usually they would be exciting for the participants the first few months, struggle for existence two or three more months, then languish and die. But I was persistent. For some reason I kept trying.

Five years after I left one of my pastorates I met a former small-group participant at an evangelistic rally. At the time I had been her pastor she had been trying to rear two teenagers on a waitress's salary. Life was a struggle. A few weeks after she invited Jesus to be Lord of her life, I asked her to join a small group. After some shakedown, there were only two other women who remained as members. I met with them enough times to get them started.

In the few minutes we had to talk, I learned that she had become active in the church and was now chairperson of the evangelism committee. After reporting about her current ministry with enthusiasm, she said, "You know, at the time we didn't think we were doing much in that Bible study, but when I look back I realize that's what got me locked into the faith."

Because of their deep need for mutual support, these three ladies had stuck together, learning and applying biblical principles in their lives. They weren't alone in the need to bear one another's burdens. Almost every Christian I knew ran into tough life problems. Why hadn't the others stayed in groups long enough to reap the rewards of rich fellowship and growth in Christlikeness?

In the summer of 1975 I learned the answer I had been looking for. It was so stimulating that it cost me a night's sleep. My family was combining our vacation with attendance at a Christian conference at Lake Junaluska. One of the seminars was taught by Howard Ball, president of a fledgling ministry called Churches Alive.

In his introductory paragraphs Mr. Ball quoted Matthew 28:19-20: "Go and make disciples of all nations, baptizing them in the name of the Father and of the Son and of the Holy Spirit, and teaching them everything I have commanded you. And surely I will be with you always, to the very end of the age."

"If you listened carefully," he said to the twelve or fifteen persons, mostly pastors, in attendance, "you will notice I misquoted that passage. I left out two words. What are they?"

Silence. So he misquoted it again. This time we had been tipped off. Still no one got the answer. By now several Bible carriers had whipped out their books and were looking it up. He waited. Finally someone got it. "To obey," he said.

"To obey," repeated Ball. "That's right. To *obey*." His emphasis at that moment didn't strike me as very significant. Then he went on to explain, and I got excited. I saw the missing link at last.

"We assume," he continued, "that when people are learning what the scriptures teach through sound biblical preaching, Bible study groups, and personal study we have done our job. But *knowing* biblical principles doesn't produce disciples. *Obeying* them is what counts."

One of Ball's many memorable statements was that thousands of Christians across our country are "educated beyond their obedience." He went on to describe a simple program by which to *hold people accountable* for putting what Jesus taught into practice.

Now I understood why Jesus and Wesley had successful groups and I didn't. Jesus held his disciples accountable for doing what he was teaching them. Wesley's class meetings were famous for checking out how well the members were following biblical precepts. Sure, there were burden-bearing and sharing of needs. But there was also an accountability factor. It's not either/or but both/and.

The reason "to obey" hadn't seemed significant to me at first mention was that I had been corrupted with the following misapprehension. Churches are voluntary organizations. There are plenty of places, like school and work, where you "have to" do what they tell you. *If people are held accountable not only for learning biblical information but also for living it out in their relationships with one another and the Lord, they'll just quit*, I thought. I discovered how wrong I was. Many Christians are eager to grow in Christlikeness so they can better serve the Lord.

Discipling isn't for everyone, but it's the primary way for Christians to break through into the joy and meaning of life in the Spirit. When others see radiantly changed lives among those who do commit themselves to supporting one another in learning to love and obey the Lord Jesus, some will want that kind of life for themselves.

At Central there are numerous small-group experiences available other than the discipling program. Koinonia groups are always necessary in a church that provides love-one-another ministries. Any number of reasons may keep persons from fitting into the discipleship mode at various stages of their lives. A church that is making the love of Jesus known will attract many people whose problems are far too deep to enable them to function in such a group. They must have loving acceptance in groups that are not pressing ahead but are willing to stop and wait or even back up a bit in order to help someone with needs. Such groups may ebb and flow, begin and discontinue. No matter. Start some new ones. Find a different program. Back off and regroup. Just make the small group ministry available.

Growing Up

The more I learned about discipling, the more I understood why helping people find their gifts and related ministries was so difficult. We don't know what our gifts are until we grow up.

When our daughters were very small, my wife taught them to make pictures with crayons and colorful paints. The pictures were fabulous. They appeared in coloring books, behind little magnets on our refrigerator, on my bulletin board, and in letters to grandparents. All four of those little girls danced and pirouetted to our delight. They would all be artists and dancers.

They are grown now. I don't think any of them dance. Two of them have artistic talent. All of them have numerous gifts we didn't know about when they were growing up. This is true in natural life, and we discovered that it has its counterpart in spiritual life. Spiritual gifts were also more likely to be properly identified in persons who are spiritually mature.

We taught that spiritual gifts and ministries, like natural talents and skills, were usually discovered and developed by experimentation. A track coach might think that one of his hundred-yard-dashers had potential as a high jumper and ask her to try it. A pole vaulter could decide he would prefer the two-mile run, but he wouldn't change events without getting approval from the coach.

We began to work out ways for our saints to explore their potential for operating in a variety of gifts and ministries. We spiritualized everything in order to be prayerfully intentional about finding the leading of the Lord. I thought it was God's church, and God wanted to direct it. Our job was to follow the injunction of Matthew 6:33. We paraphrased it like this: "Try to find out what God wants you to do, and do it. God will provide the resources."

We taught that the purpose of spiritual gifts was to build up the body, that every one of us had gifts, and that all of us were responsible for functioning under authority. The lines of authority progressed through leaders, staff, and the pastor to the ultimate lordship of Christ, the Head of the Body.

The plan was to enter into covenant for ministry in that particular area where you believe you may have a quickening, a call, a sense of being "raised up." You shared this information with the person who had leadership responsibility for that particular ministry. The leader informed you of the requirements for that work. Both of you continued in prayer until there was agreement that this was a leading of the Lord.

On the other hand, the initiative may come from leadership. Like the track coach who thought his dasher could high jump, a staff member may think one of the youth workers should be in the puppet ministry. After confirmation in prayer, he would approach the youth worker with a complete description of the task and the requirements for it and ask him to pray about it. They would come to an agreement on it, remain in waiting for confirmation from God, or decide that they didn't believe it was in God's plan to make the change.

If there was an agreement that this seemed to be the leading of the Lord, they entered into a covenant on it. For us, a covenant meant there was mutual understanding of the job description, the kind of support the worker could expect from the leader and other workers, and the belief that this was in the will of the Lord.

We believed that the Lord had provided the Body with all the resources we would need to function in God's will. It was up to us to find and follow God's way. This was the key to a Body that moved in the freedom and harmony of vibrant health.

We also encouraged our ministers to step out of their positions when they no longer believed these were God's calling for them. We taught that the Lord had someone for every job. If you stayed in it when you didn't belong, you were depriving others of the fulfillment God had for them.

The responsibility flow chart moved up through the pastor, purportedly to the Lord. I thought the mind of Christ was more likely to be discerned by a group than by the pastor alone, although he or she always had to remain singly in authority. So we sought the Lord's leading to bring together a group of people with whom the pastor shared concerns. They bore my burdens and held me accountable for my growth in Christ, as well as provided holy insight into the way our Lord was leading his church. We were on our way to loving one another, to becoming a healthy body.

I still believed an intentional ministry of healing was the heart of a healthy body. It was time now to introduce it at Central.

SO FAR . . .

- We discover the reason many laypersons are bored with the church and find little joy in their faith is that they have not realized they're called into cooperative, Spirit-empowered ministry with Jesus Christ.
- We suspect that one of the most important statements of the charismatic movement is the laity telling the church and clergy that they want a piece of the action, freedom to manifest the gifts of the Holy Spirit in worship and ministry.

- We take special note of the importance of the gift of discernment so that worship services do not become show places for personal ego.
- We agree that God's New Testament plan for making known the life and love of Jesus is to manifest God's reality through Spirit-filled laypersons in a healthy Body of Christ.
- We see the pastor's responsibility to help Christians mature in the faith, discover their gifts, and be equipped for ministering in the stream of the Holy Spirit.

For Reflection and Discussion

1. The author believes that a primary function of the pastor is to equip the laity for ministry. Among your circle of Christian friends, is there a desire for the level of Christian maturity that would qualify them to be in ministry? What are some of the ministries for which laypersons are gifted? What steps are under way toward equipping the laity in your church? Can you suggest others?

2. Are you aware of situations where a church was strengthened by an influx of charismatic renewal? Did it cause any problems? If so, why? Have you seen evidence of charismatic excess that disrupted church harmony? How could it have been avoided?

3. The homogeneous unit principle states that churches are more likely to grow if they cater to persons of like theology, interests, and goals. What strengths do you see in this theory? What strengths are there in diversity? Would you be able to worship comfortably with a variety of worship styles? How well do members of your congre-

gation accept people of varying backgrounds and theological positions?

4. The author speaks of "bearing one another's burdens
and holding one another accountable." Can this be done
effectively in churches in our society? Do you think the
average church does a better job of bearing one another's
burdens or of holding one another accountable? Cite
examples of each that have come to your attention.

5. The author states that the key ingredient for discipling
(often called spiritual formation) is in finding ways to
hold people accountable for growing toward Christian
maturity. How has this been accomplished in your own
life and/or the lives of Christians you know? Do you agree
that small groups are the most effective means for accomplishing this goal? What other means do you think of?
How willing are the Christians in your circle of friends to
be discipled? What benefits for the ministry of the laity,
particularly the ministry of healing, do you see in this
goal?

CHAPTER 6

A Marriage of Models

Distorted Expressions of Faith for Healing

By the time I had been at Central Church a year I was again eager to begin an intentional ministry of healing. The challenge here was at the opposite end of the spectrum from Wesley Church. There we dealt mostly with lack of information about healing and skepticism about its validity. At Central Church the problem was more a matter of correcting misinformation. Much of the parish accepted the validity of the ministry of healing. The trouble was that some of their ideas were couched in unrealistic or distorted terms.

Prayers for healing at the Sunday morning services had become occasional rather than the norm. However, they continued at Bible studies, prayer groups, and meetings in homes. Unfortunately, from my point of view, some valid scriptural principles, when overemphasized, became counterproductive. Distortion, sometimes disaster, was the result. There were three emphases that particularly disturbed me: the "name it and claim it" variety of positive faith; the pressure of manipulation; and the theory that illness was merely a symptom of unconfessed sin. Although these ideas were not widely accepted by church members, they continued to be expressed by some individual persons and small coalitions. Their practitioners usually were sustained by involvement in other groups outside the church where these positions were emphasized.

It was common in those days to have people tell me they had claimed the healing of their eyes. They had quit wearing glasses. Some of them said they could see better. It was a miracle. A few weeks, maybe only days, later you would notice that they had begun wearing their glasses again. Others threw away medication only to purchase a new supply when the symptoms controlled by the medication became too uncomfortable.

One distressing example was forcefully presented to me. Flashing red gumballs on a police squad car is an extreme way to represent Terry's bald head when he got angry. The resemblance was there though. He was powerfully built, an ex-football lineman, now a high school track coach. Terry's gumball was slowly flashing, pink to dull red and back again, when he came to my office.

He wanted to vent his anger about the events that occurred at a youth meeting his son and a friend had attended at a recently formed storefront church. The ministry of healing had been undertaken by some of the leaders and young people. They taught that the Bible says, "By his wounds you have been healed" (1 Peter 2:24). Underline *have been*. That means it has already been accomplished. All we need to do now is confess faith in the promise of God to receive the healing. To confess faith means believe *now*, even if you experience no improvement. *Claim* your healing, and act as if you are healed. Lingering symptoms must be disregarded.

Jeff was a tenth-grader who had an astigmatism. He had worn glasses since the age of six. He didn't want to wear glasses. He was told Jesus could heal him. They prayed mightily for him and told him he was healed. They said he didn't need the glasses any more, but Jeff still couldn't see without them.

As Jeff rode to school on his bicycle the next morning he decided to *really* believe. He threw his glasses away. Terry's son went with him to hunt for the glasses. They found them, but they had been run over and destroyed. He couldn't do his school work that week.

Jeff's parents were divorced. He lived with an older brother in poor economic circumstances. Terry bought Jeff new glasses—and he was angry.

Was it wrong to have confident faith in God for healing? Of course not. But it is wrong to dictate to God by presumptuous disregard of symptoms how and when God is to actualize the healing. Positive faith is great. To try to psych people up to demonstrate faith is nonsense. It's manipulation. It's a denial of God's precious grace.

An even more devastating form of malpractice occurred to Kim Lawrence. Kim, who began attending Central Church a few years ago when she returned from the University of Illinois, has dermatomyositis. She uses a wheelchair much of the time.

Otherwise, she walks with the support of someone on whom she can lean.

In Champaign Kim attended a fundamentalist church that taught it was not God's will for people to be ill. If they were, it could only be because they were out of the will of God. In other words, they were living in sin. Their ministry to Kim was to try to help her discover what her sin was, so she could confess it, be forgiven, and be healed.

Hearing her story brought back the same anger I had experienced one evening while watching a healing rally on television. The evangelist was preaching to a huge crowd of people in a public arena. The front row of spectators was a line of distressed people seated in wheelchairs.

I began to be uneasy as he strode back and forth, mike in hand, waving and shouting about the ravaging effects of sin. In one mighty surge of energy he raced to the edge of the platform, pointed his finger at various anguished wheelchair occupants, and shouted, "When are you going to give up your sin and rise up out of those wheelchairs forever!"

Kim was a tenderhearted young woman who felt hurt and confused by this approach. She knew they were wrong but didn't know how to rebut them. It has taken months for her to regain her sense of value in the eyes of God and God's people. We believe Kim is being healed, but the damage done to her greatly delayed rather than advanced her experience toward salvation, healing, and wholeness.

The scriptural rationale for this approach is found in the story of the paralytic carried to Jesus on a pallet by some friends (Luke 5:17-26). Jesus demonstrated his authority to forgive sins by first saying to

this man, "Your sins are forgiven." When the Pharisees questioned in their hearts whether Jesus had
that authority, he continued, "That you [that is, the
Pharisees] may know the Son of man has authority
on earth to forgive sins . . . I tell you [the paralytic]
get up, take your mat and go home."

There is no question that sin can and does lead to
emotional and physical illness. But it is not the only
cause. To make it so only confuses issues. The result
is devastating to the personalities of precious people
who struggle to discover what sin may have caused
a wrathful God to inflict disease upon them.

Some of the laypersons who endorsed the ministry of healing continued to see it in terms of instantaneous change, primarily in the realm of the
physical. Furthermore, they disdained the idea of
an established time for exercising this ministry, because it "put God in a box," instead of giving God
freedom to heal whenever God wished.

A pastor with this view once half facetiously told
me his wife asked him when he planned to begin
having services for healing. "Never," he answered.
"What if somebody gets sick on Thursday morning,
and your healing service is on Wednesday evening.
You've got to wait a week before you can pray."

Because of prevalent attitudes such as these and
the understandable revulsion of many parishioners
against these teachings, the mindset at Central
Church was more of a challenge in which to inaugurate the intentional ministry of healing than that at
Wesley Church had been.

Francis MacNutt sees the problem this way in *The
Power to Heal.*

Some recently formed Pentecostal churches and groups, frequently the victims of an anti-intellectual bias, have preached universal healing, without complete balance but with great effect, while the established churches, proud of their intellectual tradition, have preached on the subject of healing with great caution but little power.

Somewhere there must be a way of speaking which is courageous in its faith but true to reality.

At Central Church we set out to try to find out what the Lord would have us do about an intentional ministry of healing and do it. By this time I had been their pastor eighteen months. It pleased me that so many Central members believed God had not become locked out of natural processes. They knew spiritual power was available through faith. It remained for us to find together the ways best suited to maximize the effects of God's healing love among us.

I saw the task of education as twofold. On the one hand, we had to continue to disavow all kinds of manipulation, emotional hype, and false expectations. On the other, we needed to elevate the theology of the cross. What God has done in Christ overshadows in significance the miracles we may experience by highlighting the gift ministries of the Holy Spirit.

I identified a list of about forty people who had demonstrated energy for the ministry of healing. These were people that I had seen or heard about praying for others to be healed. They each received a letter from me asking them to pray for the Lord's leading in regard to the future of the healing ministry at Central. They were invited to meet together at my home on Friday evening.

Expectations, especially mine, were high as the people began to arrive. Most of those invited had come. Only one key leader was unable to be with us, and he had called with obviously sincere regrets over his unavailability, pledging support for our plans.

I had asked Greg to bring his guitar to help us in our time of worship. We began to sing praises to God. I felt the peace and joy of God's presence, even a sense of God's approval, as if God were telling me in advance that this was the way to go. The quietness of the prayers, the holiness of the worship, the depth of seeking the Lord gave us the feeling that we were in God's will. The saints were clearly ready for me to share with them where I believed the Lord was leading us.

I began by telling of my own healings, what I had seen in Houston, and the miracle of Gene Harbison. It seemed God's anointing was upon us. Benign expressions glowed at me from loving faces around the room.

Wrapped in the enthusiasm of good memories, I described the Sacramental model for an intentional ministry of healing, *a la* Wesley Church. I explained the necessary minor adaptations that would fit that model to Central. I waited expectantly for positive feedback. I waited a long time in the silence.

There was no anxiety about the silence, but I began to suspect the rapt attention that was given to my presentation was more an eagerness for the subject of healing than appreciation for my "how-to" lecture. My hidden agenda, propose a service of healing in which the pastors did the honors, was different from theirs. I sensed that some of them were thinking that the pastor is finally coming around to approve healing the way we used to do it.

Someone broke the silence by reminding the group of a highlight experience. "Remember the healing services John Wesley Fletcher held at the Masonic Temple? Wow! People being healed right and left!" Murmers of agreement all around. Two or three private conversations were being carried on around the room, evidently telling how great it was.

Someone else said that, like the pastor, he had also been healed of high blood pressure. It had happened while a soloist was singing "The King Is Coming" one Sunday morning at Central. Even as I had fondly remembered Wesley Church's entry into the ministry of healing, so there continued a series of additional fond reports of miracle days at Central.

A spirit of thanksgiving and praise was upon us. Someone voiced it in prayer. Greg led us in "Praise the Name of Jesus." More prayer. I said the Lord was blessing and guiding us and asked if they could return next Friday evening to continue seeking God's way for the ministry of healing. Then I offered a benediction, and my wife served refreshments.

As I reviewed my notes and feelings from that first meeting I gave thanks to the Lord for lay ministry. Here in our experience together a new style of pastoral leadership was emerging. At Wesley Church I had proposed the model for healing and carried it out. At Central we—pastor and laity—were discovering together the model of healing ministry the Lord had for us in our particular expression of the Body of Christ.

Five more Friday evenings we met for prayer and praise, discussion and mutual learning. They learned that Sunday morning worship was not going to revert to one long miracle-seeking service, though I acknowledged the possibility that there might on occasion be such an anointing that we would have no choice but to go that way. I learned that the ministry of the laity meant their perceptions of how these services should be conducted was at least as instructive as mine *and* that the laity should be in the forefront of such ministries—what I had claimed to want all along.

Week after week we were surprised by and we rejoiced over new insights, new agreements mending former differences. I taught directly and vehemently against the name-it-and-claim-it and all-illness-caused-by-sin theologies.

At the same time we agreed on the value of positive faith and the fact that sin always causes devastation in human life. We emphasized that the focus of faith must be not in healing, not in a method of healing, not in someone with the "gift" of healing but in Jesus Christ, the only one with power to heal.

We were also in agreement as to the importance of celebrating the Lord's Supper for cleansing from sin and for centering faith in Christ, the Redeemer and Healer. In this context we emphasized that salvation is not completed in one experience but that it is an ongoing process toward wholeness.

The Lord's plan for all people is that they be made whole in body, mind, and spirit. Our discussion of the process by which God makes us whole, enlightened by Leslie Weatherhead's definition of healing in *Psychology, Religion, and Healing* as the restoration

of "the broken harmony which prevents personality
. . . from its perfect functioning in its relevant environment," broadened the understanding of the
ministry of healing for several of the participants.

We discussed the manipulative aspects of giving
rote wording to those being prayed for with instructions to parrot it back. We gained a deeper sensitivity to the potential danger of playing God. It
became obvious that to superimpose any of the
various fad theologies or healing formulae in all
situations would be foolish and probably counterproductive.

Time after time I swallowed my chagrin over having misjudged the practices I had heard were being
exercised. I learned those had been occasional and
sometimes reported out of context. The intimacy
born of our worship, prayer, and open discussion
established deep mutual trust. The ministry we
planned required teamwork. We were beginning to
become a team.

In this model for an intentional ministry of healing the clergy would lead in the Sacrament of Holy
Communion. But the laity would be instrumental in
manifesting the gifts and ministries of the Holy
Spirit for healing. Nothing had been lost from the
Sacramental model. Something holy and equally
important had been added in terms of Body Life. We
called it a marriage between the Sacramental and
the Body Life models of healing ministry.

Our plan was to hold a weekly Communion and
Healing service. The service would begin with an
informal time of praise and worship, including testimonies, a brief homily on one of the healing episodes of Jesus or the Book of Acts, and the

celebration of the Lord's Supper. To this point the service was not unlike that of Wesley Church.

Following the Communion service, instead of having the pastors pray for those who came forward, we would have teams of laypersons anoint and pray for them. Certain persons who had been identified as being in covenant for this ministry (as described in the previous chapter) would be in the worshiping congregation. I would designate teams of three, each one made up of both men and women, to come forward. These teams I would anoint for the ministry of healing for that evening.

While this was being done, the congregation would sing a hymn. Then they would be invited to come to one of the praying stations at the altar, describe their need, and receive anointing, laying on of hands, and prayer for God's remedy for their situation.

During this time of ministry, I was available for consultation where needed, to sit with persons quietly in the pews, and to oversee the service. There were rare occasions of disturbance when it was necessary for me to be available, which I would not have been had I been praying at the altar. Instead of feeling left out by not being one of those anointing and laying on hands, I knew I was fulfilling the proper role.

A few years later I wrote a project dissertation on this ministry in partial fulfillment of the requirements for a doctor of ministry degree. One of the members of the examining committee before which I made my oral defense evidenced disdain bordering on hostility over this practice of healing. He asked me why we had laypersons rather than pastors pray for healing. As I began my explanation of the need for someone to be in charge of the service, he abruptly interrupted, "I submit, sir, that you do not pray for them, because you're afraid your reputation will be damaged if they are not healed."

"Not at all," I replied. "Everyone we pray for is touched by the healing love of God. Not all of them experience it at the time. Some leave feeling untouched, though most walk away in the glow of God's presence. However, that part of it is God's business. Our business is to express faith for what God wants to accomplish, then trust God for the results."

In addition to the pastor and prayer triads, the healing team required people for four other kinds of ministries: helpers (ushers, Communion stewards, and someone to monitor the sound system), those present for praise and worship, intercessors, and musicians. All team members were asked to consider themselves called to this ministry and to see themselves as channels of faith through which God's healing love would be free to flow as God wished.

During the time of altar ministry there would be quiet music, usually a soloist or a duo singing with guitar accompaniment. From time to time worship choruses would be sung. Those in the congregation who desired to do so were encouraged to sing along. Meanwhile, the designated intercessors would be praying for the persons at the altar.

We agreed that team members would arrive fifteen minutes before the service for a time of prayer and spiritual preparation. About once a quarter we would meet following the service to update our education, discuss and pray about the way the services were going, and decide on changes that needed to be introduced.

It was our desire not to dominate the church with this ministry but simply to make it available. We agreed there would not be a heavy promotional emphasis. We wanted people who desired to be a part of the healing ministry to take advantage of the services. Others would not feel they were sabatoging the church program if they didn't support this ministry by their attendance.

For purposes of education and encouragement for our church and healing team, we planned to invite a well-known writer or practitioner in the ministry of healing to lead a healing mission at Central each autumn. We would set aside one day of this mission for a clergy workshop for pastors who were interested in learning more about the ministry. Our list of leaders includes Donald Bartow, author of *The Adventures of Healing;* Tommy Tyson, widely known United Methodist evangelist, retreat director, and charismatic leader; Charles Boleyn, leader among United Methodist charismatics in Georgia; Francis and Judith MacNutt, authors of the influential books *Healing* and *The Power to Heal;* Dr. William P. Wilson, for many years a professor of psychiatry at Duke University and author of *The Grace to Grow;* and Larry and Audrey Eddings, United Methodist evangelists from the Seattle area.

The Communion and Healing services were scheduled to supersede the regular Wednesday evening Bible studies at Central. For a twelve-week period prior to our launch date, which was Ash Wednesday, 1981, we would undertake a Bible study on the healing love of God. In addition, I would preach several Sunday morning sermons on the theology and practice of the healing ministry at Central.

I had stressed two ideas during our preparatory sessions. One was that we should broaden our understanding of healing to include more than the physical. I frequently told the group that whenever you say "healing," let the word include in your mind salvation, healing, and wholeness of body, mind, and spirit.

The other theme was intended to lift the burden for results from human shoulders and place it in the hands of our sovereign God. I put it this way: perfect love plus perfect faith produce perfect wholeness. I explained that *perfect* in this context meant "complete."

Perfect love and perfect wholeness were God's domain. Being perfect love, God has expressed that love completely through the death of Jesus on the cross for our reconciliation and redemption, including body, mind, and spirit. God, who alone can produce perfect wholeness, is working out that salvation in us until "the Day of the Lord."

The other term in the formula, *perfect faith,* is the cooperative part God invites us to play. Faith does not produce healing. Expressed faith is the channel through which we receive the healing love already poured out through the atoning work of Christ. Human beings do not express faith (or anything else) perfectly. However, to the extent that we focus our faith for healing in Christ, his salvation, healing, and wholeness enter our lives to our well-being and the glory of God.

An exciting sense of joy and enthusiasm permeated that first Ash Wednesday Communion and Healing service. We felt the presence of God, especially in the flow of quiet worship and the deep quality of peace.

Hope

James said faith without works is dead (2:17). Try this one: "Faith without hope is dead."

Those who have endured suffering for a long time will be either overshadowed by despair or sustained by hope. If despair prevails, the life of faith will soon fade into the shadows with hope. From there it will die in the darkness.

Paul spoke of rejoicing in suffering. He wrote of its being the forerunner to perseverance, character, and hope. The result of this hope, Paul said, was that the love of God floods our hearts by the presence of the Holy Spirit (Rom. 5:1-5).

The difference between despair and hope dawned in my consciousness one day about a year after faith in Christ had become a reality for me. I had just become the pastor of a small-town church. I fixed up a room in the church for a study. My plan was to work there each morning. In the afternoon I would visit members of the parish.

Right after breakfast I went to my desk. It was B-Day, the Beginning of a new kind of life. I was eager to live it well.

Out came the books for sermon preparation. I began to read. Within minutes I was feeling drowsy, an escape symptom that had plagued me through years of continual depression. Before long, I put my head down on the desk and slept till noon.

The next morning the same thing happened. Once, barely awake, I thought, *O God, I'll never make it if this happens all the time.* Those years of dull, gray despair which had canceled initiative and kept me helpless came to mind. In that moment I realized something new. I was not always going to be this way. Maybe today. Maybe tomorrow. But not always. I had hope.

In the old days I would have succumbed to the pattern, believing there was no way out. Now I knew there was hope. Yes, I was depressed. True, I didn't know the reason, but that didn't matter. I knew that Christ would bring me out of it, and that made all the difference.

Paul indicated in one of his prayers that the Holy Spirit has power to produce hope in the lives of believers: "May the God of hope fill you with all joy and peace as you trust in him, so that you may overflow with hope by the power of the Holy Spirit" (Rom. 15:13). Multitudes of suffering Christians whose healing has not been manifest have waited not only with faith but also with hope.

Joni Eareckson was paralyzed from the neck down in a diving accident while still a teenager. People all over the world prayed for her healing. Through years of faith struggle she learned that God had not forsaken her. She began to think of her healing as delayed, but she had hope.

> The peace that counts is an internal peace, and God has lavished me with that peace.

And there's one more thing. I have hope for the future. The Bible speaks of our bodies being "glorified" in heaven. In high school that was always a hazy, foreign concept. But now I realize that I will be healed. I haven't been cheated out of being a complete person—I'm just going through a forty-year delay, and God is with me even through that.

"God is with me even through that!" When faith is thought of primarily in terms of a trust relationship with a person, the immediacy of the "you *have* what you believe" is fulfilled in the intimacy of God's presence. That is the supreme healing. Relief from the symptoms of distress for which we pray may then be more a matter of hope than faith, although I grant that this could be an unnecessarily fine distinction.

Furthermore, our understanding of the healing process includes the realization that the malignancy may be near the end of a chain of cause-and-effect relationships intertwined through spirit and emotions with the body. Think of the game of pick-up sticks. At the bottom of the pile is the red-tipped stick you would like to retrieve. However, to get that stick without destroying the pile, you must slowly and carefully remove numerous other sticks.

Perhaps there are situations in which the ailment that we pray for to be healed requires that a number of other healings of spirit and mind are first accomplished. The Divine Healer alone knows the stages of healing and the benign sequence which must be followed to reach that particular need.

Part of faith is to trust God for that knowledge.

When answers to prayers of faith seem to be delayed, we continue in hope. Doubtless there are healings accomplished all along the way, some of which are never evident to the hurting person.

Consider this hypothetical situation. A man has received confirmation of the suspected diagnosis of a cancerous growth in his colon. Afraid that this may prove to be fatal, he comes to the healing service for prayer. But there are a number of other anxieties, separate causes for hopelessness, that stir his mind. Who will love his wife when he is gone? How will she be strengthened during his illness? Can he still work during treatment? What will happen to his income? Is there adequate health insurance, or will his family become penniless? Does this kind of cancer cause more pain than he can bear?

If the prayer of faith brings him into loving union with the Lord Jesus, hope springs alive. He may not have the healing he desires, but his despair over many areas of concern has been replaced with hope. His body, mind, and spirit have been relieved of numerous tensions that would have served only to block an easy flow of God's healing power, both medically and spiritually.

There is for all of us, whether in robust health or physical anguish, an inward "groaning" as we wait for the "redemption of our bodies" (Rom. 8:23). Those who are ill have a more distinct consciousness of this interim time of waiting. It is a time of outward uncertainty but inner assurance; for the witness of God's Spirit that we are God's heirs, co-heirs with Christ, alleviates our suffering.

Hope is ours. In Paul's words, "For in this hope

we were saved. But hope that is seen is no hope at all. Who hopes for what he already has? But if we hope for what we do not yet have, we wait for it patiently" (Rom. 8:24-25).

Many of my friends have lived with this hope through months of suffering. Proponents of the "God wants everyone miraculously healed" school sometimes disdain the idea of death being God's ultimate healing. But there is more to entering that mysterious realm beyond brain wave and heartbeat measurement than Elizabeth Kuhbler-Ross's stages of dying (helpful as they are in describing the process) can fathom. There is a gracious difference between the experience of those who live toward expiration in the hope of ultimate healing and those who have no hope.

Steve Downey was not healed of cancer in this world, but he was made whole in the most complete sense; that is, in body, mind, and spirit. Once he became aware of the "love of God . . . shed abroad in our hearts by the Holy Ghost which is given unto us" (Rom. 5:5, KJV), his whole demeanor changed. There was an aura of love, joy, and peace about him, even in times of severe pain.

The Saturday before Holy Week we talked together. He had been moved to a private room. Steve reminded me that God loved him just as God loved Jesus, and Jesus had suffered. He said it was good to know God's love.

Then he said, "Reverend, I want to go home." Steve hadn't been back to the farm for over two months. He wanted to be with his family, away from the activities of the hospital, in his own bed. But in the reality of his intimate faith-union with Jesus, we both knew he now had a double view of where home was.

I took his hand in mine to pray that his desire would soon be granted. "You will be, Steve," I said. "You'll soon be home."

The phone at church rang just after the benediction the next day, Palm Sunday. Someone was calling from the hospital to let me know Steve had just died. I drove right over, arriving within the hour. I knew his parents were waiting in the family room, but I went straight to Steve's room.

I stood looking down at Steve for a long time. No one else was in the room. His face was pale and thin, but there was an undeniable expression of peace on it. Hope was not disappointing. He had gone home.

Five years after beginning healing services at Central, Tom Brown invited me to speak at a church in another city where he was chairperson of the board of elders. At the time of our first healing service he had been a member of Central. "I thought that was a great service," he said, "but I had no idea they would continue year after year."

I thought they would. The atmosphere of faith in Christ is strong and contagious. People feel love from one another. Many who have never experienced it before come away knowing for the first time a deep sense of the forgiving, healing love of God. Few who attend fail to sense a quality of peace that is rare to find.

As months of experience, evaluation, and testimony passed, I realized that what was happening at this altar and in these pews was the ministry of Jesus himself through his Holy Spirit. He was bringing salvation, healing, and wholeness to bear in a di-

rect, white-hot way in people's lives. It seemed to
me to be at the very center of what the church was
called to accomplish.

It is the heart of a healthy body.

SO FAR . . .

• We agree that certain one-dimensional theologies
for healing, while true in themselves, become manipulative and counterproductive when used ex-
clusively.
• We emphasize that faith for healing should be
focused in Christ and what he has done and is
doing for our salvation, healing, and wholeness.
This focus is best maintained by keeping the
Lord's Supper at the center of the worship service.
• We seek members of the healing team from among
those mature laypersons who believe they are
"called" to function in the gifts and ministries for
salvation, healing, and wholeness.
• We initiate an intentional ministry of healing
which includes clergy leadership for the Sacrament of the Lord's Supper and the ministry of the
laity in music, worship, prayer, anointing, laying
on of hands, and prayers for healing. We think of it
as a marriage between the Sacramental and Body
Life models of healing ministry.
• We find participants in the healing services experiencing such a direct, peaceful, effective flow of
God's saving and healing love that we know the
ministry is a core expression of God's purpose for
the church. It is the heart of a healthy body.

For Reflection and Discussion

1. The author expresses concern over potential distortion of healing practices indicated by the name-it-and-claim-it school, manipulatory instructions for activating faith, and the all-disease-is-caused-by-sin concept. What important value for the ministry of healing do you see as a core truth in each of these distortions?

2. At Central Church the intentional ministry of healing came to be thought of as a marriage between the Sacramental model and the Body Life models of healing ministries. What values do you see in involving the laity in planning the style of healing ministry in a local church? What are the drawbacks to that method of planning?

3. The author emphasizes that healing is accomplished by the grace of God through the faith of persons. Indicate ways that faith in Christ for healing of persons can be enhanced. Tell how your personal faith has grown over the years.

4. Joni Eareckson is quoted as speaking of a delayed healing, "I have hope for the future." Try to verbalize ways in which faith and hope are similar and/or dissimilar. Do you know of someone who draws strength from his or her hopefulness?

5. What are some of the ways the pastor and laity of Central Church sought to discover the leading of the Lord for the intentional ministry of healing in that church? How do you find God's will for your life? What are some practical steps your home church could take to discover whether or not an intentional ministry of healing is appropriate at this time?

EPILOGUE

A Church That Is Learning to Love

Years ago I made an important discovery. Bob and Sarah had just left my office. I was sure they felt worse after the session than when they had arrived. They still loved each other, but their relationship had deteriorated to criticism and carping on her part and silence on his. Each of them explained changes the other needed to make in order to be a proper mate.

As I jotted some notes about their comments in my file I thought how healing it would be for the relationship if they could just back off a little. They needed to express love for one another. Then they would be freed from the defensiveness that interfered with any change taking place. *How can I help them to know that?* I asked.

This thought starter came to mind for our next session. "It's our business to love people and God's business to change them." I don't recall that this was any great help to that couple, but it certainly gave me something to think about.

"It's our business to love people and God's business to change them." The typical church plan for changing Christians into the likeness of Jesus is to command them, on the authority of scripture, to do so, then apply enough peer pressure and fear to force the change. It isn't working very well, because—whether we realize it or not—most people put up emotional defenses against such a barrage. They may change outwardly, but internal change is the goal.

This "new" thought of mine is anchored in the belief that the Holy Spirit is always at work in Christians to change them. When we cooperate with the Spirit in faith and obedience, changes occur. When we resist, we're miserable. The misery comes not from pressure applied by other people but by the absence of community with God.

The Body of Christ can radiate love and acceptance. Such a setting provides the atmosphere of emotional support that frees persons to face reality about who they are. They can drop their defenses, pretenses, and (as sometimes needed) the psyched-up Christian glaze that overlays their real character. Then the Spirit of God has free entry to carry out a remolding project.

Paul told the Ephesians: "Be kind and compassionate to one another, forgiving each other, just as in Christ God forgave you. Be imitators of God, therefore, as dearly loved children and live a life of love, just as Christ loved us and gave himself up for us as a fragrant offering and sacrifice to God" (4:32-5:2).

A recent phone call from out of state illustrates the resistance this idea has aroused. This good friend of mine has found a "dynamic Bible-believing church" to attend. He has enjoyed the rapid growth of the church and wants to help me with what he thinks of as a more scriptural perspective. "This loving and caring is not where it's at. Changed lives is where it's at. What counts is changed lives."

This was Paul's goal, too. He told the Galatians he would keep experiencing birth pangs until Christ was formed in them. "Loving one another" does not mean people aren't held accountable. It means they're never condemned. They're always accepted as they are, not forced to meet others' standards in order to be acceptable.

There are times to "speak the truth in love," but the church has erred more on the side of speaking the truth in authority than in love. I acknowledge, of course, that it's not love to allow people to go on living in sin without helping them find repentance and forgiveness. It's not either/or but both/and. It seems that Jesus began with individuals by loving and accepting them.

"Changed lives is where it's at." I'll buy that. But people who don't know they're loved have serious difficulty changing. The church's great challenge is to be able to express the kind of self-giving love that Jesus did. Scott Peck, in *The Road Less Traveled*, gives us a clue to the reason for this:

> On the other hand, children who are truly loved, although in moments of pique they may consciously feel or proclaim that they are being neglected, unconsciously know themselves to be valued. This knowledge is worth more than any gold. For when children know that they are valued, when they truly

feel valued in the deepest parts of themselves, then they feel valuable.

The feeling of being valuable—"I am a valuable person"—is essential to mental health and is a cornerstone of self-discipline. It is a direct product of parental love. Such a conviction must be gained in childhood; *it is extremely difficult to acquire it during adulthood* [italics mine].

It is our experience that a significant proportion of the people with problems who come to our healing services, indeed, to our church, would benefit from an increased sense of value, of feeling loved. Evidently there are plenty of human beings around who missed out on the parental love Peck says is so essential to mental health.

These people are not usually helped by being told they have to change. They already feel unloved and without value; they see themselves as failures. They will try one more time if enough pressure is put on them. But sooner or later they will just disappear unless they somehow perceive that love and acceptance are available among these Christians.

There is no doubt, as Peck says, that it is extremely difficult to acquire this feeling of being valuable in adulthood. The *only* context I know about for receiving the kind of love that would make that possible is a "loving one another" Body of Christ.

Just as God the Father manifested love in human experience by sending Jesus Christ in the flesh, so this love must be somehow enfleshed. The only people I know about who have enough love in their own lives to do that are those about whom it was once said, "See how they love one another."

Since my parents were intent on loving me, I don't know why I grew up without appropriating that love. Nevertheless, that has been and is being overcome by experiencing God's love and acceptance through God's people.

Moroseness, anxiety, irritability, and depression were no infrequent companions of mine. Hope and determination kept me going. My rationale was that a little minor pain was no reason to be canceled out. Christ was my strength and my redeemer. At the same time I continued in hope for further healing as I lived "by faith in the Son of God who loved me and gave himself for me" (Gal. 2:20).

In the summer of 1977, my wife, Marie, and I were among the forty-seven thousand conferees in Kansas City at an interdenominational charismatic conference. One of the seminars was on healing of the memories and was led by Ruth Carter Stapleton. I had read extensively in that field because of my interest in psychology and my ongoing search for more complete mental health.

One of Mrs. Stapleton's teaching methods was to lead the entire group, hundreds of us, through the healing of memories procedure that she employed. I well remember the melancholy fog that settled on me as we were led to reconsider hurtful events at various stages of emotional development. The instruction was to reexperience each one in our imagination, picturing the presence of Jesus and inviting him to heal the hurt. This didn't seem to work for me.

The next summer we were at a Baptist charismatic conference in Green Lake, Wisconsin. There I met someone who made a practice of ministering in the

field of inner healing and made an appointment
with her. She led me privately through an exercise
similar to that of Mrs. Stapleton with the same apparent lack of result. For some reason this method
was not getting through to me. I put it on the back
burner and left the idea there for future reference.

*If I could jump up and down, shout, scream, pound on
the table, swing from the chandelier or do ANYTHING
else to get the reader's attention for the MAJOR MES-
SAGE of this book, I would do it now!* I wasn't ready in
my unconscious mind to face the changes being
offered by the spirit of Jesus for inner healing. I
didn't realize it at the time, but I felt too insecure to
risk healthy change. Only when love and acceptance through a group of relatively mature Christians convinced me of my value was I able to allow
myself to face certain deep needs for healing.

At a time of stress, frustration, exhaustion, and
minor depression I asked a Christian friend to lead
me once again through a pattern of prayer for inner
healing. As in the past I apparently received no
help.

The next day in prayer I was reminded of that
unsuccessful venture. Suddenly a picture was
formed in my mind of an old familiar room. It was
the dining room with the heavy rectangular table,
legs bowed and knobbed, at which we all ate dinner
during my first five years of life. "We all" meant two
great-grandparents, two grandparents, my mother
and father, two adult aunts, and several other older
adults who took room and board at my grandparents' home during those years.

A little boy stood alone in the room by the table.
Slightly shorter than the table, he looked up

wistfully, as if—though there was no one there—to gain the attention of those seated around it.

He felt alone, forlorn, abandoned. He wanted someone to care for him, to love him, but no one noticed him. He felt deeply wounded. More than anything else, the little boy in the picture felt sorry for himself. I was that little boy.

A little boy stood alone in the room by the table. Slightly shorter than the table, he looked up wistfully, as if—though there was no one there—to gain the attention of those seated around it.

He felt alone, forlorn, abandoned. He wanted someone to care for him, to love him, but no one noticed him. He felt deeply wounded. More than anything else, the little boy in the picture felt sorry for himself. I was that little boy.

I don't know if this image was a replica of an actual occurrence or not. It was a distinct truth about a previously unidentified, but deep, strand of my emotional programming. That little boy was still in me, feeling that same forlorn sense of deprivation.

Self-pity, unrecognized as such, was a controlling influence in my life. Not only was it unrecognized; it was also firmly denied. I liked to think of myself as strong and courageous, driving ahead in the midst of emotional adversity, giving no quarter to inner pain. What a deception!

Self-pity, which I so detested in others, was my own sin. Try as I would to package that feeling as sin and repent of it so I could be forgiven and free, it slipped and slithered away from me. It was a hurtful fact of life. I decided to treat the problem as a traumatic wound, subject to the healing power of Jesus Christ.

During prayer time at the next Wednesday evening Communion and Healing service I knelt at the altar before three trusted friends and said, "I need to be healed of self-pity." This was probably no revelation to them, but they made no comment. Gently, with acceptance and compassion, one of them anointed me on the forehead by making the sign of the cross with his forefinger dipped in oil. Each of them prayed for God's healing love to accomplish the healing I requested.

For several months I knelt before members of the healing team each Wednesday evening with that same request. "I need to be healed of self-pity." No condemnation ever was indicated. I experienced nothing but love, acceptance, and fervent desire that the healing release the Lord and I were moving toward would come quickly.

Months later the Lord brought me to the place where I was strong enough to give up this dear, sick little boy. I had been working on a sermon theme from a favorite verse: "I want to know Christ and the power of his resurrection" (Phil. 3:10). It appeared to be easy to develop, but I was stymied. As I sat in a back pew one Wednesday evening playing that verse through my mind, the thought came, *You can't give positive thrust to that great idea unless you include the rest of the verse.*

O.K., I thought, *but I had wanted this sermon to be tremendously upbeat.* Nevertheless, I pushed on in my mind to the rest of the verse: "And the fellowship of sharing in his suffering, becoming like him in his death." In those moments I moved away from the sermon to my own sin. I had no further need, as I identified with the suffering of Jesus on

the cross, to hold on to my own childhood suffering.

The very next opening at the altar found me saying to the prayer team, "Jesus has healed me. I've
come to give up my self-pity for the sin that it is." I
confessed my sin, was anointed for absolution, and
walked away free.

Being absolved of self-pity does not mean that I
have never since felt sorry for myself. It means that
when I do I recognize my self-pity for what it is,
confess it, turn from it, and go on in faith. Prior to
the healing, I still needed self-pity as a crutch; it was
my sick way of dealing with hurt. Now I was well
enough to handle the situation realistically. It was
the love of the Body of Christ that made it possible
for the Lord to work this change in my life.

One of the criticisms we occasionally hear about
the ministry of healing is that the same people go
back week after week and never get healed. It's true
that there are numbers of severely traumatized persons who soak up this help every week. Without it
they would not be able to function at all. The Lord is
strengthening them, one area at a time, each pick-
up stick in sequence, until they become whole.

There are times when it is the leading of the Lord
to tell people in no uncertain terms about their sin.
But conviction of sin is clearly the work of the Holy
Spirit, not of human analysis. If the Spirit chooses to
accomplish that convicting work through the prayer
team, so be it. More often the work is done in a more
internal way.

Networking is an important feature in the "loving
one another" makeup of a healthy Body. It is comprised of members with a great variety of gifts and

ministries. Many of these are of a social nature. Others are in the various committees and task groups that perform outreach or inreach ministries. This network, of course, includes the staff and pastors.

Susan came to Central about two years ago. She struggles with feelings of unworthiness and insecurity. Since joining Central she has attended a K-group (koinonia) and the Barnabas Fellowship (a singles ministry) with regularity. Still, she always seems to be by herself.

Every Wednesday evening Susan sits alone at the Communion and Healing service. I always slide in beside her and give her a hug. Usually someone will go sit with her for a period of time. She seems to like that. Near the end of the service she goes to the altar to receive prayer ministry.

About a year ago I invited her to consider having a Stephen minister. A Stephen minister is a layperson trained to meet for an hour each week to listen and support persons who are going through difficult stages of life.

One afternoon I returned to my office a few minutes prior to a scheduled appointment. My secretary told me Susan had been waiting for over an hour to see me, even though she had been told I might not be available for very long. Susan was agitated. She told me she had had nightmares the two previous nights, dreaming that people from our church had died. Last night she had been awakened by the dream, had turned on the light for a while, and finally had gotten back to sleep.

The first night the dead person had been a child. The second night it had been an adult. In the dreams she did not see the people. She saw their caskets being carried and knew who was in them.

I told Susan that sometimes dreams are insignificant, sometimes they give us information about our inner lives, and sometimes the Lord is using them to speak to us. I asked her which of those categories best fit her dreams. She said she didn't know, but it was obvious that these were not insignificant dreams. I told her a way to follow up on interpreting the meaning of these dreams was to be prayerfully quiet before the Lord and listen to see if anything came to mind.

After a time of quietness I asked her if anything had come to mind. Her response was more definite than anything she had said until then, "Yes. I didn't know Don Hadden had died until after he died." (Don was a member of our church who had died of cancer a few months earlier at the age of fifty.)

"You mean a long time after he died?" She said she found out about it the evening of the memorial service. "Did you know Don well?"

"Yes, but I know his children better."

"Are you about the same age as his daughter?"

"Yes, a couple of years older."

"Are your parents alive?"

"My mom is."

"How long has your father been dead?"

"Seven years."

"Did he die suddenly?"

"Yes, in a car accident. It was on May 24." That day was May 25.

"Were you getting along well with him when he died?"

"No."

"Do you feel you could have done more for him than you did?" She nodded, almost in tears.

"Let's pray about it. Let's ask the Lord to forgive us for any sins we might have." I prayed a brief prayer to prepare our hearts for repentance. I told Susan to ask for forgiveness. She asked the Lord to forgive her for the use of alcohol, rebelliousness, and "everything else I did." I made a statement of absolution.

I asked Susan if her dad loved her and whether he knew she loved him. She said he loved her. "No, my dad didn't know I loved him. I never acted like it."

I suggested to Susan that she think of a place where she and her father would be in comfortable surroundings and to see both of them experiencing Jesus' love together. I reminded her that Jesus had forgiven her and told her she should ask her father to forgive her, too. I told her that her dad would certainly forgive her and feel good to hear her say she loved him.

Then I asked her to dramatize this scene with me by putting her arms around me just as if I were her daddy, telling me she was sorry, asking me to for-give her, and telling me, as her stand-in father, that she loved me.

When she put her arms around me, I hugged her to me as tightly as I could. She told me she was sorry, asked forgiveness, and said she loved me. Then she smiled broadly. I said I understood her, forgave her, and had always loved her.

Apart from the months of experienced love and acceptance Susan had received from the Body Life model, she would not have had the strength to walk in, suffer the long wait, and receive the ministry we shared together. The heart of a healthy Body, pumping the healing love of God through its members, is producing salvation, healing, and wholeness of body, mind, and spirit in God's people.

APPENDIX

Principles for an Intentional Ministry of Healing

The Heart of a Healthy Body includes stories about two extremely different local churches, each of which came to inaugurate an intentional ministry of healing. The resultant models are distinctive; neither would function effectively in the other church. The basic principles learned from the experience of these two churches are outlined here in the expectation that they are applicable to a variety of local church settings.

1. **Preparation:** *Be careful that no surprises are sprung on the congregation.*

The congregation should be given at least six to eight weeks advance notice of the "exploration" of the ministry of healing. Some members of the congregation will probably resist this ministry. Polarization will be less likely if such advance notice is given.

If possible, the pastor should provide one or more sermons on the subject. Everyone who has an interest, pro or con, should be encouraged to attend the sessions investigating the possibility of inaugurating these services.

2. **Exploration:** *Approach the intentional ministry of healing as an adventure in discovery.*

To live by faith is a challenging adventure. It means, for one thing, to continually seek the leading of the Lord for the direction of the church. Do not take for granted that every church requires an intentional ministry of healing, that there is a common model for all churches, or that this is the time for an intentional ministry of healing in any given church. Such a ministry might, however, be worth considering, since Jesus put so high a priority on healing in his own ministry.

The author describes the discovery process for two churches. In the first, the church experimented with a plan called "Exploration in Spiritual Healing." Persons convinced of the value of such a ministry were called in to describe their experiences; a panel discussion was held; a "trial" service of healing was held. This "exploration" was evaluated and became the basis for regular monthly services of healing. The pastor took the lead and planned the services.

In the other church, a series of meetings was held with parishioners interested in the ministry of healing; the pastor offered a weekly Bible study on the subject; sermons were preached explaining the biblical theology for such a ministry. The group worked together with the pastor to plan the liturgical format for the intentional ministry of healing.

This preliminary "exploration" phase may be initiated by either the pastor or laity, though never without the pastor's willing involvement. There should be as broad a spectrum of parishioners as possible involved in this discovery phase. A prayerful conclusion dismissing the idea may be as valid as one advising the initiation of the healing ministry.

3. **Adaptability:** *Launch the intentional ministry of healing as an experiment.*

Once the decision has been made to begin the ministry of healing and an appropriate liturgy has been chosen, there will be eager anticipation on the part of those who are involved. The initial plan, however, may need some rather immediate revision. The plan developed on paper should be experimental, subject to improvements that may become obvious when the ministry is actualized.

4. **Focus:** *Keep the theological focus of the ministry in the healing love of God as expressed and activated through the Son, Jesus Christ.*

During the time of preparation and planning, those involved may have a tendency to focus more on the persons and the format for the ministry of healing than on God's healing love flowing through human agency and utilitarian methods. Always remember that God is the source of all healing. This healing love is supremely demonstrated and activated through the saving grace of God manifested in the crucifixion of Jesus Christ. Therefore, it is strongly urged that each healing service be centered in the Eucharist, which tends to keep our faith focused not in healing nor in someone designated as a gifted healer nor in one or another method of healing, but in the life-giving death of Jesus Christ on the cross and his subsequent resurrection.

5. **Faith:** *Emphasize the importance of faith to be exercised by each person without sacrificing integrity.*

There are many different understandings of what healing is and how one expresses faith to receive it. Do not insist on too narrow a definition of healing (it should include healing of body, mind, spirit, and relationships) or of limited ways to express faith. All healing comes by the grace of God and is received by faith. God's part is grace; our part is faith. It is paramount, therefore, that we emphasize the need for exercising faith and that the focus of faith is in God rather than in the method of faith's expression.

6. **Lay Ministry:** *Involve as many different qualified persons as possible in the intentional ministry of healing.*

In the ministry of Central Church, there is a team comprised of persons who lead worship, serve as ushers and helpers, prepare the Communion elements, engage in unobtrusive intercession from the pews, and pray for those who directly request the ministry of healing. These persons function together as a team and understand their role to be part of the Body Life expression of the ministry of healing. Team members may be chosen at the initiative of the pastor as he or she evaluates their maturity and giftedness for this work, or they may request consideration for involvement in this ministry. In either case, the resulting agreement between pastor and layperson should be understood as a calling in response to the Lord. The commitment should be to God for the work of healing rather than to the ministry itself.

7. **Responsibility:** *Provide careful pastoral oversight of the ministry.*

The ministry of healing is one of the more sensitive areas of spiritual care in our churches. It is important that persons on the healing team be mature and stable Christians, trained in the theology and practice of the healing ministry. The pastor must take responsibility to oversee this process.

8. **Versatility:** *Be sensitive to the need for variety and the possibility of change.*

Over a period of months, the service of healing may tend to be satisfying and accepted as valid without considering modifications. When you begin to experience the cumulative benefits of an intentional ministry of healing, there will seem to be no need for changing the approach. Perhaps no change will be necessary but methods for considering the need for change should be built in in advance.

9. **Maintenance:** *Provide low key ways of keeping the ministry healthy.*

From the beginning we have understood that the intentional ministry of healing beats, like the heart, internally. It is behind the scenes rather than the tail that wags the dog. Nevertheless, like each other ministry of the church, it needs a degree of visibility to the congregation in order for parishioners to take advantage of its benefits. Furthermore, there is need to maintain the size and quality of the healing team and to give opportunity for persons new to the church or new to the vocation of healing team ministry to become involved in it.

10. **Results:** *Be sure that God, the source of all healing, rather than the participants or the ministry, gets the credit for benign results.*

"To God Be the Glory" is not only the title of a song; it is also the purpose of the church and certainly of the intentional ministry of healing. Much resistance to the ministry of healing stems from the distaste that occurs from apparent self-exaltation of proponents of the ministry. Avoidance of this problem is lodged in full recognition, in spirit as well as in word, that the healing ministry is part of the salvation work of God through Jesus Christ. That spirit of humility is the result of worship of God as the source and sustainer of all healing.

About the Author

Herbert Beuoy is directing pastor of Central United Methodist Church in Decatur, Illinois. He has received the degree of Bachelor of Divinity from Garrett-Evangelical Theological Seminary and the degree of Doctor of Ministry from Asbury Theological Seminary. He has been the pastor of several churches in Illinois since 1961.

Before accepting his call to enter the ministry, Dr. Beuoy had a varied career, holding positions as a teacher, a bank clerk, a caseworker for families with dependent children, and the proprietor of a bowling alley. Dr. Beuoy has four children and five grandchildren.